Left Standing at the Fence is a journey of survival through abuse. The author is sharing her story of how she has overcome many years of trauma from the one who is supposed to be our most trusted and nurturing person in our life. Abuse comes in so many forms, and we don't even recognise it ourselves until it is too late. I admire the way the author has risen above all of the trauma, recognised she needed help, and sought the help she required. And I also admire her ability to look back and realise that there were many moments of happiness she could grab onto.
Rita-Marie Lenton
Celebrant
Author *Creating a Fond Farewell*

The journey of this Soul has taken its toll on a long and arduous road, that many sadly have given up on. We see just how painful it has been for Donna— is it any wonder she has had to struggle to find her place and her reason to live? Abuse is an awful and sad reality of life, especially mental and emotional abuse. Donna deserves our respect, compassion, and love for recognising she needed to reach out for help, and for facing her lifelong difficulties. Happily, Donna had the shining light of her Dad to guide her initially, and I am so glad she had the overarching example of Pop and Nana T to show her what real love is. Donna's friends, Brian and Carlie, are the epitome of friendship, and stuck by her to show her what love can achieve. It is devastating when a child's soul is crushed time and time again through life's experiences; however,

Donna is to be praised for her determination, courage, and strength. It is my opinion that any one of those souls who have been abused would find strength and purpose in what she's overcome, and the efforts she has put in to find healing—on an ongoing basis. All the very best, Donna, on your healing path. Dad would be proud!

Marnee Kent
Author *Dreams, Visions & Intuitions – Awaken to the Call of Your Own Innate Power*

Left Standing At The Fence

A Survivor's Story

Of Abuse

Donna Daffurn

Left Standing At The Fence
Copyright © 2023 Donna Daffurn
First published 2023
Revised edition 2024

Disruptive Publishing
17 Spencer Avenue
Deception Bay QLD 4508
Australia
WEB: www.disruptivepublishing.com.au

Front Cover by Deborah Fay, Disruptive Publishing
Back Cover image and title page image
by April Werz Photography *aprilwerz.com*

All rights reserved. Without limiting the rights under Copyright reserved above, no part of this publication may be reproduced, stored in, or introduced into a database and retrieval system, or transmitted in any form or by any means (electronic, mechanical, photocopying, recording or otherwise) without the prior written permission of both the owner of the Copyright and the above publishers.

ISBN 978-0-6457459-4-8 Print
ISBN 978-0-6457459-5-5 EBook

DISCLAIMER

This book is a memoir, written entirely from *my* memories, based on *my* opinions, and only *my* opinions. This book is *my* experience of the world.

No malice is intended to any person mentioned in this book.

Some names have been changed, due to privacy or legal considerations.

CONTENT WARNING

Left Standing At The Fence is a vivid memoir, where childhood memories are interwoven with present day recollections of a difficult and complex family life. **As a consequence, this book includes elements that may not be suitable for some readers:**

- strong, coarse language
- death
- violence
- marginalisation
- trauma
- mental health issues

Readers who may be sensitive to these issues please take note.

Thank you to Brian, my best and closest friend,
Thank you for all you do for me.

To Sky, my Mental Health Clinician,
and Olivia, my Wellbeing Consultant,
both of whom have listened to me and seen my tears.
Thank you for everything.

Table of Contents

ONE | Context 1

TWO | 1962 to 1968 5

THREE | 1968 to 1972 15

FOUR | 1972 23

FIVE | 1972 to 1974 35

SIX | 1974 43

SEVEN | 1974 to 1976 52

EIGHT | 1976 63

NINE | 1977 75

TEN | 1977 to 1981 81

ELEVEN | 1983 to 1991 93

TWELVE | EARLY 1991 103

THIRTEEN | LATE 1991 107

FOURTEEN | 1993 to 1997 113

FIFTEEN | 1998 to 2002 119

SIXTEEN | 2002 131

SEVENTEEN | 2003 to 2005 141

EIGHTEEN | 2005 to 2006	149
NINETEEN | 2007 to 2008	153
TWENTY | 2008 to 2009	161
TWENTY ONE | 2009 to 2010	171
TWENTY TWO | 2010 to 2011	177
TWENTY THREE | 2012 to 2013	183
TWENTY FOUR | 2013 to 2014	191
TWENTY FIVE | 2017 to 2022	199
TWENTY SIX | 2023	207
TWENTY SEVEN | Reflections	211
ABOUT THE AUTHOR	219
ACKNOWLEDGEMENTS	221

ONE | Context

This book is about *my* memories of abuse, the trauma that comes from that abuse ... and much more. It is all *my* memories. No one else's memories. It also shows how I survived through something that is so common—and yet so hard to comprehend as an abused child. Attitudes regarding disciplining children were different when I was a child, and today some of that *discipline* would be considered abuse: physical, verbal, and mental. I would like to be more specific about the abuse that I received and suffered, as a child and through to my adult years but unfortunately for legal reasons I can't say more.

SO, what is a mother?

A mother is one who loves you, cares for you, and teaches you all you need to know for the life that is ahead of you. Plus, other little important things.

Well, that is what a mother is supposed to be, or do.

Ha! Ha! In my case it couldn't be further from the truth. My mother was not a *MOTHER to me*.

I went from being a child growing up with a family, to living in a broken home, and then losing the man who was my rock, my best friend, the man I laughed with—

my Dad. In my childhood, teenage, and adult life, I endured physical, mental, and emotional abuse from the one person every child should be able to rely on for unconditional love — her *mother*. Without that love and support I needed in my life, I had to find ways of surviving without the life skills that a mother would normally teach a daughter.

The many health problems that I have endured are also illustrated throughout this true recollection of my life.

SO why write this book you may ask? I was seeing a mental health clinician and, after hearing everything I had suffered and been through, she suggested that I write my life story — my memoir. I started, then a person stopped me — yes, **Maree** — so the book was put on ice for a while. Then one day much later, one of my mental health team suggested that I continue writing my book so my voice could be heard.

First and foremost, maybe, just maybe, my story could **help others to heal as well**. If someone reading my story could be *saved* from abuse — or whatever they are going through regardless of what it is — or could see there is life *after* abuse then my book has served its purpose. Also, I hoped breaking the silence of abuse — not only for me, but for others — might help me to heal. And it has to a degree; it is a long journey, but I am willing to take it.

Left Standing At The Fence

My story shows that, against all odds, I have survived assault and abuse, not only from my mother, but from my children and extended family as well. And if reading my book helps just *one* person to know they can survive abuse and move forward with their life, then writing my story will have been worthwhile.

I didn't think I could get through it all, but I reached out and received help, and even to this day I have counselling to help me get through life.

But I have survived!

If I can survive what I have gone through, then I know others can as well **... it starts by reaching out for help.**

TWO | 1962 to 1968

I was born in 1962 at the Nambour General Hospital. The eldest of three children to Dad, Ron, 22, who worked as a labourer, and Maree, 22, who was a trained nurse. They named me Donna Maree; Dad wanted a boy. I don't recall my birth weight or measurements.

Dad, Maree, my Great-Grandma, and I lived in my Great-Grandma's house—well it was more of a shack—but it was home. The shack was in the suburb of Parklands, north of Nambour on the Sunshine Coast in Queensland, Australia. We lived there until sometime around 1963 when we moved into a home in Nambour Heights. The house in Hillcrest Avenue had a great big backyard, which backed onto a swamp and the soon-to-be constructed bowls club—more about that shortly.

In 1965, three years after me, my two sisters—Sandra and Wendy—were born. Maree did not know it, but she was having twins. There were no ultrasound scans back in those days.

Maree stayed at home looking after the three of us. Our grandparents, Con and Olive Daetz, (Maree's parents) did not live too far from us, and they owned the last shop between Mapleton and Nambour, on Mapleton Road, Nambour Heights.

Pop and Nana were well known around Nambour Heights because of the store, and they would assist anyone who needed a hand around the whole Nambour Heights area and towards Mapleton. You could say they were local legends and were well respected for their service to the community. In addition to giving help wherever it was needed, Pop and Nana were active members of the Nambour Orchid Society — Pop served as president of the society during this time — Pop was involved with the Nambour and Maroochy District Band, and he was well known to the Maroochy Shire Council.

The Nambour Heights Bowling Club was established in 1967 as a result of the efforts of one man in particular, my Pop, Con Daetz. Nambour Heights was developing rapidly in the 1960s, and Pop believed there was a need for a bowling club at Nambour Heights, in addition to the one in Nambour. Pop donated the land and guaranteed the building loan for the construction of the club. Most of the construction work was completed through working bees, where the men, including my Dad, helped Pop build the club and the green. Additional funds were raised by holding raffles. The green and clubhouse were officially opened on the 7th of December 1967, and in the early 1990s the bowling green was dedicated in his name. [1]

Additionally, the Con and Olive Daetz Park in Isabella Street, Nambour Heights, is named in honour of my Pop and Nana, and it is a fitting tribute to their many years of supporting the local community.

To this day, Nambour Heights Bowls Club maintains the clubhouse and the green dedicated to Con Daetz, and the Sunshine Coast Council cares for the *Con and Olive Daetz Park*. Both entities deserve recognition and acknowledgement for preserving these tributes to my grandparents.

Nana and Pop's shop has changed hands on many occasions since they sold it. The old store still stands today, although I am not sure what the building is used for. Their modest house on the block next door also still stands, and as a building it is just memories for me now. Even though their old house has been renovated, it is still Nana and Pop's house to me.

Our house in Hillcrest Avenue was close to Nana and Pop, the hospital and, of course, the bowls club. When we were young, Maree would help at the shop. Behind the shop was a big shed that had all the stock for the shop, as well farm supplies and stock feed, and equipment for the farmers who lived around the area.

---

[1] Additional information courtesy of Nambour Heights Bowls Club website | https://nambourheightsbowlsclub.com.au/our-club/

The milkman would come to the house and deliver milk in glass bottles. The garbage man would pick up the bin and empty it and bring it back. The good old days!

There was a house up the street from us, but below us there were only a few houses and a lot of empty house blocks. These were the early days of Nambour Heights.

Quite often, Dad would go *walkabout*, now it is not as bad as it sounds, it was only around to the neighbours for a beer or two. I was supposed to stay home, but not this black duck, where he went—I went. I remember clearly that many an argument started with Dad visiting the neighbours.

I do not remember doing much with my sisters, or about my sisters' lives, during this time and up to 1972.

Growing up we had a dog, a purebred dachshund named 'Lady'. She was so protective of my sisters it was not funny. Dad got bitten one day going in to pick up one of the twins. Despite this, 'Lady' lived a long and happy life!

Now, being a hardworking man, Dad started extending the house. And one day he ran into a nail that was sticking out of a post. Well, Dad let out a few choice words—and at the time I did not understand them—so down to the hospital he went, and Nana and

Pop looked after us. If Maree and Dad had something on then Nana and Pop normally took care of us.

School was a little different back in my day, we started with kindergarten, then went on to Infants School, then State School, and then finally on to High School.

Back then there were three terms each year separated by a short break at around Easter time, then two weeks holiday in May, and again in August, and then six weeks holiday at Christmas.

I remember only little bits of kindergarten. I went to the local kindergarten; we had our little bottle of milk at morning recess, and we had a sleep on camp-type beds in the afternoon. We did hand painting, outdoor activities, and we went on 'field' trips. Life could not have been better.

After kindergarten, I was off to 'big school', as we called it. Nambour State Infants School consisted of grades one through to three. When I started Infants School, Dad started driving the school bus that picked up children from the Kureelpa and Dulong area west of us. I remember sitting in the front seat of the bus right up near my Dad, looking at the cows and saying 'hi' to the farmers and all the different people we passed—everyone knew me by name.

Now Nana and Pop grew all sorts of the most beautiful orchids, and I still have a picture of me next to a big pot of flowering orchids, it is a photo I cherish.

I always loved the beautiful scent of Nana's and Pop's orchids, and today the delightful fragrance of those blossoms reminds me of many happy times: being with Nana and Pop, my first wedding, and my late Aunty Carol's wedding. Of course, my Nana was doing all the floral arrangements for the wedding, and I was the flower girl; there were no bridesmaids, just me. It was life come full circle that years later Carol's daughter, Joy, was my flower girl for my first wedding.

I had long blonde hair, so long I could sit on it. So, on the morning of Aunty Carol's wedding we were down to the hairdressers. Well, after a long time I had two hundred bobby pins in my hair, they used three large cans of hairspray, and at last my hair was finished. I had rings of hair from the top of my head, then around the back of my head and then on top of each other.

I wore a green dress with new, white shoes. The shoes hurt my feet because Maree would not let me wear-in my new, white shoes before the wedding. I remember walking up first in front of Aunty Carol. My next memory of the day was later that night taking all the bobby pins out. Well, it hurt having Maree brush my hair. The pain was so bad I was in tears. So, she tried washing my hair, after about five hair washes, using all different stuff my hair was somewhat straight. Never again! I loved my long hair.

We did not see much of Aunty Carol, as she had been working and living in many different places. I never liked Uncle Bill, her husband. That is all I will say about him.

My Dad, Ronald Keith Lawlor

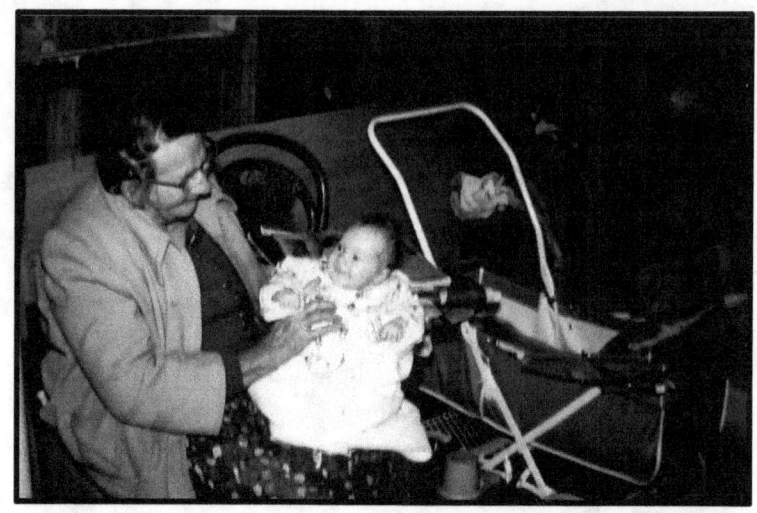

Great-Grandma and me

Dad, 'Lady', and me

Left Standing At The Fence

In my younger years, happy

Aged four, with my grandparent's big potted orchid

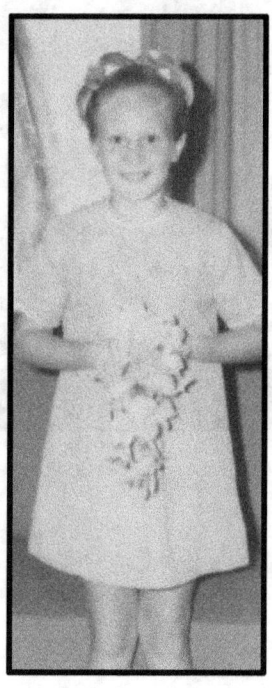

Flower girl for Aunty Carol's wedding

THREE | 1968 to 1972

Dad drove the school bus for a few years, and then he stopped. Next thing, Dad is driving a big truck with a trailer. This was in 1968 or 1969, or thereabouts. This started his many years of truck driving. I do not remember much of his first truck, but his second truck I remember well. It was a big, red International with the 'Brambles' sign on top.

Dad was away a lot. I do not remember much of these years, but I do remember I missed him *so* much. Maree returned to work at the hospital. Then in 1969 we moved; Dad and Maree had sold the house and bought a farm up at Mapleton. Oh, it was so much fun, at the start! Dad got pigs and cows, and grew some types of beans. My bedroom was on the end of a sleepout. The kitchen had a wood stove and, yes, the loo was outside.

The house and farm were right next door to the Mapleton State School principal's house, and the school was only two doors down from the farm. There was a huge tree behind the house, which we were not allowed to climb. The farm went from Mapleton Road, all the way back to Obi Obi Road. We were not allowed to run on the farm without an adult with us. There was no milking machinery in the dairy, so we only milked the cows by hand. The cows were out-of-bounds to us girls, unless an adult was with us.

We should have been living a good life, but with all the restrictions on us life was hard. When you are a child, you naturally want to run and investigate things. Every afternoon we had chores to do, and one of them was to bring in wood for the stove. No wood, no stove, we got no hot water.

One day Dad built a pen for the calves, near the dairy. Oh my, the pen was full of lantana and stinging nettle! Then Dad bought a Brahman calf. We looked for that bloody calf all over the farm, around Mapleton, and through people's farms on the east side of Mapleton. Three days later Dad found the mongrel in a huge lantana bush on the east side of Mapleton.

Well, let us say it did not stay on the farm long—off to the sales yard! Dad was still driving trucks, and Maree had returned full-time to work. Life was not that great. Dad was home for a day, and then gone. When he was home it was all yelling and doors slamming. Dad did drink a bit; other people may have a different opinion on that.

Dad had a mate who drove a log truck. Holy hell, could he drive a truck. He put a truck and trailer in places no one else could! He had a green Mack with a trailer, and he hauled logs for the Mapleton Sawmill. To this day, I believe he is the only man to have brought a load of logs up the old, precarious Obi Obi

Range. Halfway down the range, on the Obi Obi Road, there is a rock wall where a line used to be gouged out of the rockface by that load of logs.

Now, the range is about halfway between Mapleton and Kenilworth. Obi Obi is just farms with a community hall, no shops, etc., well it was back when I was young and lived out at the 'Obi', as we called it. It's a very scenic drive through many farms, until you reach the intersection which will take you on to Kenilworth or back to Eumundi. Originally the range was both ways, up and down. Now, after all these years, and many people crying out for safer travel on the range, the roads have been improved. The George Wyer Scenic Drive now crosses the Obi Obi Road, and the road down the range is separate to the road up the range. Driving either up or down the range travellers drive on part of the Obi Obi Road *and* part of the George Wyer Scenic Drive. To get a better understanding of how this works, and how dangerous the original road was, look it up on Google Maps. According to Google, the only death I can find that happened on the range was way back in 1938. Way before my time.

Caravans have tried to go down the range, but they would invariably get stuck and block the road until the caravan was moved on. Dad and his mate struck up a good relationship, always talking about trucks, and working on trucks.

When Dad was home he would go down to the pub. And many a night Maree would be mad, because Dad was drunk and had been at the pub all day. Now, from the pub to home was only four doors away. It went: the pub, the rest area, the school, the principal's house, and home. Once, I got into trouble for something that happened and so my rear end felt Dad's hand, and when his hand could not reach me, his foot did. By the time I got home, I was in tears and sore. Looks like Dad is going on the road again! More yelling and doors slamming.

One night the phone rang late, which was unusual. It was the police. Dad had been involved in an accident at Proserpine, or so we were told. He was alright; he had sore feet and a few scratches. We were told that Dad had pulled off the road to check the load of steel on his trailer. At that time, I think he was hauling for Thomas Nationwide Transport (TNT), and apparently another truck hit his truck head-on, on the corner of a hill.

Now remember, this is what we were told, and as the years have gone on, I have doubted how correct this information was. Many years later I drove on the highway around Proserpine, and there is nowhere that the accident could have happened as the police described it. So let's say it happened somewhere in Queensland.

Dad was supposed to be getting better by not walking much, but he was either down the road at the pub or across the road. Across from us lived a family that had two adult twins. Dad was friends with them and often when he was home, he would spend time with them. After a few weeks, Dad bought another truck. Maree had encouraged him to buy another one at the cost of $21,000, requiring him to go into debt. Another International, this time painted orange and white, the TNT colours, and with a TNT sign on top of the cabin.

Now, one weekend Dad had to re-floor the trailer, and I was out there with him. Maree screamed at him and told him not to allow me up on the trailer, and that I should not be around the truck. But I loved it. Like most children, I did not listen, and I fell through the part of the tray where there were no boards onto the gravel driveway underneath. So of course, it hurt, and I let out a bellow.

Thankfully, Maree had already left for work that day. She worked different shifts at the hospital; if I remember rightly it could be: day shift from 6 a.m. to 2 p.m., afternoon shift from 2 p.m. to 10 p.m., and night shift from 10 p.m. to 6 a.m. I think the times are right, but it *has* been a long time.

School was not much fun, and the Mapleton School was small compared to Nambour. There were four grades in the one room. I can remember being bullied at that school, and going home in tears to no understanding or help. Maree said, "Just go and do your chores." It was about 1970 when the twins started school. I do not remember much else, other than the big *do* on them starting school a year earlier than they should have. Remember, things were different back in the 1970s.

We had different 'babysitters' or 'housekeepers'. I can recall one woman, who lived at Montville. She was a great woman. I remember her helping me with my homework, and we would walk around the farm together. She had a kind heart. Then she left to get married, so we had another woman come and take care of us. Maree put an ad in the local paper for a babysitter/housecleaner, and Tracey answered it and got the job. When Tracey came to look after us, she was a young girl herself, only sixteen years old. She started on the 10th of June 1972.

I cannot remember too much of what we did or how I felt then. In 1972, all the furniture, the farm, the tractor, the cows, the pigs, etc., were sold at auction. I remember everything out in the front yard being auctioned off. Dad had been away a lot, and later in life I found out he had been in Townsville, and he had either bought or rented a home for us to live in. So everything was sold at the auction. My life on a farm was gone. No more running through the paddocks, going down to the smelly pigs or carrying in firewood. No more dance lessons and competitions won with Dad. It was one thing Dad and I enjoyed. Maree even made me a new dress for the one and only competition Dad and I entered and won. Life was about to change, and I did not realise just how much that would be.

Left Standing At The Fence

Dad's red truck with the Brambles sign on top

FOUR | 1972

In August of 1972, Maree, me, and the twins drove to Townsville; Dad had already gone back up there.

The car Maree drove at that time was a white Valiant station wagon. Compared to today's cars it was a tank! It had no seat belts or air-conditioning, and you had to wind down the back window by hand.

Nana and Pop Daetz were also travelling with us with their campervan. Now Pop was very good with his hands, and he had made the camper himself. I don't remember the trip, but Tracey also travelled up with us.

The home, well it was different! The house was located in the suburb of South Townsville, right opposite a yard which, back then, had shipping containers in it. This was *so* different to Nambour or Mapleton.

The house was built high off the ground, with a huge bathroom, large lounge, and a sleepout where us three girls slept. My bed was placed right up towards the front of the house. The windows along the eastern side of the house were all louvers. The bathroom, oh I have never seen one like it again! You could run around and around in it; it was so huge. The shower rose was attached to the ceiling at one end of the room, and the loo was inside as well.

Off we go, to South Townsville primary school. It was so close that we could walk to school. Some days I remember Dad coming and walking us home. At that time Townsville was nothing like it is today. We would walk everywhere, go out to play, and never get into trouble. But yet again, I had no friends.

Dad was working taking bridge girders up the Harvey Range to the Greenvale Nickel railway line that was under construction. Well, Dad could drive, and he knew what he was doing getting the bridge girders around the corners. If you haven't done it, you don't know the skill involved in doing the job. The difficulty Dad faced in taking the long girders up the range, well let's say he knew his job and was bloody good at it.

Other drivers at the time need the same praise, as the job was not an easy one. They were all very skilled men and knew what they were doing. Pat on the back to every one of them.

I cannot remember the name of the suburb where the girders were made, but Dad would go there and load up the truck, and then do the trip up the range.

One day sticks in my mind. I was about eleven, and Dad took Tracey, my sisters, and me in the truck when he was taking a 60-foot girder up the range.

Apparently, with girders of this size, the rear of the girder has to be winched around the corners. Now when dad took a 60-foot girder up the range, a work mate would be with him, and that mate would be the one winching the rear of the girder around the corners.

Now, I was a young child, life was great, and I was as happy as could be. Dad told us we had to stay in the truck when we started going up the range. Off we go, we get up a bit and then Dad stops the truck. I think nothing of it. About halfway, Dad was on a corner and his mate was winching the rear of the girder around, when Dad called me to his seat.

"Have a look out there," he said. Oh my goodness! Talk about scared. To this day I do not know how that truck managed to stay on the road. What I saw was many trees and a long way down to the bottom. The front wheels must have barely been on the road.

To say I was terrified would be an understatement. I got out of that truck faster than a fly, took off up the range, and did not look back. I remember sitting in the red bulldust waiting for Dad to reach the top. His boss came along and sat with me until Dad got there, but I have never in all my days been so bloody scared!

One day, not long after this, I was helping Dad clean out the truck at home. I noticed the name 'Tracey' under the driver's side windscreen visor. I cannot remember Dad's response to me asking why Tracey's name was there.

At that time life was great, and I do not remember any sad times. I guess it was because Dad was home that I wasn't getting into trouble so much, and the beltings from Maree had stopped. I was more likely to be in trouble with Maree when Dad wasn't there. For once, I felt loved and wanted.

But one night my life and family changed forever ...

In Townsville, Maree was working as a nurse, Dad was driving the truck, and Tracey was looking after us girls. Sometime around the 7th of October 1972, all of us three girls were in bed. I was not asleep because of the yelling from Dad and Maree.

After a while, I thought enough is enough! However, what I saw has stuck in my head for many years now. I opened the double doors to see Tracey standing back crying, while Dad and Maree were in a heated argument which had become physical. I saw Maree's hands around my Dad's throat and I yelled, "Leave my Dad alone!".

"Go back to bed!" Maree screamed at me, and after that my memory becomes a blur. I have tried and tried to remember what happened next, but no matter what, the memory won't come back. I believe the trauma of this emotional experience has caused my memory of the violent argument to become repressed.

Next thing, I hear more yelling and the back door slam, the car start up, and Dad screaming something. Meanwhile, the twins are crying, and we are all sitting in the corner with a blanket over us. I do not remember going back to bed that night. And I do not remember any more of that night or the next day. All I knew was that Maree was out of the house. Tracey would walk us to and from school. Something was up, but what it was my young mind could not understand.

One morning we opened the front door to see strange cars parked across the road. Tracey called Dad, and next thing the police were there. Back then children weren't allowed to, and didn't, listen to adult conversations.

Next minute, Dad is in handcuffs and this big ugly copper is leading him out of the door. Well, a herd of buffalo would not have held me back, how dare they take my Dad away, "No, leave him alone!"

After that happened a policeman in a car would follow every move the three of us girls made. Writing this it sounds funny, but it was anything but funny, we were walking to school with Tracey and behind us were policemen in cars. No matter what Dad did, or we did, Maree was going to inflict hurt, pain, and trauma — especially to me.

Suddenly, Maree was at the door with the police, she had come back to get more of her stuff. According to documents I accessed from the State Archives on the 12th of June 2010, Maree only found out about Tracey and Dad on that night in October, when the shit hit the fan.

Now all this happened back in 1972, so I can't remember some of the particulars, like dates or times.

But I do have court papers showing that on the 26th of October 1972 Maree applied to the court in Townsville for custody of us girls, but the magistrate refrained from dealing with the application. Then on the 3rd of November 1972, in a court in Townsville, a judge ordered *by consent until further orders*, that the three of us were to be in Maree's sole custody.

I cannot remember the exact day when Maree came with the police to get us three girls, but I do remember hugging Dad and not letting go. It took a police officer to get me off him. I did not care what Dad had done, he was my dad and he loved me. My happy world was gone now. At that young age I did not realise what trauma and pain I was going to endure from then on.

I remember we moved to the other side of Townsville into a policeman's house, and he had two sons. He ran the Police Citizens Youth Club (PCYC) not far from the house. I can remember not wanting to do anything, and just wanting my Dad. Maree made us go to the PCYC, and I hated it; I was no good at gymnastics, or anything else. I wanted to see Dad, but Maree pointed a finger and screamed at me, "You won't see your father again!"

Nana and Pop came up and stayed in their camper at the back of the house. The adults did a lot of talking. Sometime in December, I think it was, Maree had packed up everything and we left Townsville and Dad, and drove to Nambour. I can remember somewhere between Townsville and Nambour,

Maree's car and Pop and Nana's car ended up in between an Army convoy!

Years later, I understood why Maree said, "Your father threatened to run us over with the truck and kill us!" I believe Maree made up her own version of the truth so that we would fear/hate Dad. It pissed me off, and in fact I was bloody outraged, when I eventually learned how many of Maree's stories were nothing but lies, extremely hurtful, and yet again controlling.

At some point after we left Townsville, Tracey returned to the Nambour area, and then later, around mid-April, Dad left Townsville to be with Tracey and nearer to us girls. Court documents show that Dad paid child support for us even though he was not allowed to see us.

According to information I obtained from Maree years ago, and from the State Archives, I learned that Dad was charged with carnal knowledge. To my total surprise and dismay this was something I knew nothing about. What the hell! I could not believe what I was reading. Tracey was under seventeen when everything happened and, because Maree went to the police after the fight to tell them, Dad got charged.

Dad was sentenced on the 12th of February 1973, and he spent about six months in jail, in Townsville. I have never been able to find any paperwork regarding his sentencing or his time in jail.

From evidence in the records I got, I believe the marriage between Maree and Dad was broken before we all moved to Townsville to be with him.

In Townsville, Maree asked Dad to take Tracey out, in whatever way he saw fit, as she had no family or friends in Townsville, and all she did was look after the three of us girls. Now, I really believe Maree's actions are what caused Dad and Tracey to start an affair, get together, call it what you like. Dad was a bloke, and Tracey was young and attractive. You don't need a master's degree to work out what would happen. Anyway, I believe because of Maree's encouragement for Dad to spend time with Tracey, and the already rocky state of their marriage, an affair between Dad and Tracey was unavoidable.

But the question is, why was Maree doing this? Was it her desire to control people, did she want Dad to have an affair with Tracey, or was there another reason? I don't blame Tracey for having an affair with Dad, she was young and she had little life experience. If anything, I would say good on you and thank you for making Dad happy.

From everything I read in the court documents, I feel very proud of my Dad. Through everything that was thrown at him, including all the police questioning, Dad continually stated that he wanted to see us girls. He continued to pay child support, even though he had little hope of ever seeing us again. One of his court statements confirms this: 'That wife of mine will do any mortal thing to keep me from getting my kids.' Additionally, evidence from the State Archives states Dad's belief the main reason for the marriage ending was 'Maree's continuous interest in money'.

The next photo shows Dad's last truck. Even though it is in black and white, the TNT colours were actually orange and white. In this picture Dad is securing a bridge girder to go to the Greenvale Nickel Railway Line.

Dad securing a bridge girder on his last truck, with TNT corporate colours

Above and below: Dad's truck at the girder loading yard in Townsville

Left Standing At The Fence

The last photo I have of Dad, taken in Townsville

FIVE | 1972 to 1974

When we arrived back in Nambour we lived with Nana and Pop. Remember, they lived in the house next door to the shop they used to own and manage.

Maree put a pool up in the front yard; it was round and only about three feet high. I lived in that pool, loved the water. One day I got a fright; my lovely long blonde hair had turned green! Maree never allowed me to wash my hair each night after I had been in the pool, because it was 'too much trouble'.

So now Maree washed my hair repeatedly, but it did not come back to blonde. Down to the hairdressers. I cried. My hair was cut off all the way up to the base of my skull. Think about it, the length, and how it made me feel! Nothing was said about my hair anymore, other than to wash it every night if I had been in the pool. I have never had blonde, natural blonde-white, hair again, and I can't grow my hair to the same length now.

Maree started work back at the Nambour Hospital, so Nana and Pop looked after us when she was working. She enrolled us into the Nambour State School, and she ensured that Dad was not allowed there. School life was torture, a total misery, and a living hell for me daily!! I was bullied; I had swearwords—that I didn't understand—written in my books; I was made fun of; I had no friends; I was called all sorts of names; and I was laughed at. When I would go to Maree for help about the bullying it was always, "*You* must have done something, just behave yourself, and stop causing trouble!"

So, life was lonely at school and my grades were not good, either. But one thing that I loved about school was being in the recorder band. I remember the teacher, she was an older woman; she listened to me, and would wipe my tears away after the kids had been cruel to me.

We did not see much of Dad. However, when we did, we went down to my aunt's and uncle's house at Maroochydore. I recall that my aunt ran the café at the Mooloolaba Surf Club. I remember going with her to the club and, of all things, sitting and peeling potatoes.

It's funny that to this day I hate peeling potatoes!

This was 1973 to 1974, and I remember some of the things from that time. Like when something happened during one of the school holidays. Now Pop was German, and a big man too. His hand was a lot bigger than my 11-year-old bottom. And I felt it a few times!

One morning something happened, and I said I was running away. Being from the Lawlor/Daetz family, everyone in the neighbourhood knew us. So, I did not get far until Pop was driving his car alongside me and was yelling at me to get in. I finally did get in, but I paid for it, from Pop *and* Maree.

In late 1973 Maree started building the **'family'** home in a court in Nambour Heights, on land that Pop Daetz had given to her. Maree financed the build with a loan from the Bank of New South Wales. I believe that G.J. Gardner Homes was the building company, and the date that the concrete slab was laid is etched into it.

School came and went; the holidays were the same, seeing Dad was not regular. We would get ready, and the next minute we would be told, "You are not seeing your father,".

Nana was good; she did try to teach me things. One thing I got into was orchids. As mentioned before, Nana and Pop grew orchids, and some beautiful ones at that. Nana gave me a few to start with, and it went from there.

Because Nana and Pop were members of the Nambour Orchid Society, when it came time for the annual show, it was time to polish up the sugar bowl and anything else Nana pulled out! I would help them serve sandwiches, tea, and coffee. One year I entered a display in the competition. With all the work Nana did, she still had time to help me. I won first place over the only other young person in the club. It was my first year and I won! And who presented me the prize, but

Pop!! But then I started to grow up and orchids lost their appeal.

Pop Daetz presenting me with the prize. I have no photos of Nana Daetz.

We always had to help around the house, and I do not remember the exact date, but I do remember that on this particular day someone was looking after us.

Back then, the washing machine had a wringer on top, and you fed the laundry through the wringer to squeeze the water out. It was two hard plastic or rubber cylinders on top of each other and they rolled in opposite directions.

Well, I got my little finger caught in a pair of underpants, as they were going through the wringer. I knew where the release clamp was, but I could not release it with my arm in the wringer. I finally pulled the lead from the power point and the clamp released.

Meanwhile the whole neighbourhood heard me screaming. Someone said they thought I was being killed! When I got my arm out of the clamp, it hurt so bad, it was not funny. All I could do was hold it because it was *so* bloody excruciatingly painful! My right arm had gone through the wringer from the fingers to the elbow.

I don't remember it, but someone took me down to a doctor and he bandaged it up for me and said, "No school, and don't use it for a few days."

I got home and the arm started to hurt more and more. The bandage had been put on too tight, and my fingers were going white. Someone re-bandaged my arm, and I got in trouble for it — of course — but it was just an accident.

The **'family'** home was still being built slowly, and I don't think we moved in until around April-May 1974. This house was a lot smaller than Nana's and Pop's, but I had my own room. At last, my own room, my own bed, no longer sharing a bed!

I got a three-quarter bed, which had been Aunty Carol's. I loved that bed. In the new house, I had a room, the twins shared a room, Maree had her room, and we had a spare room for the person who looked after us. It also had a lounge room, and a *very* small kitchen/dining room!

Beside the kitchen sink was the back door and that led down a staircase of twelve steps to the bottom. The front door and sliding glass door opened out onto a verandah, and then it was about twelve steps to the bottom there too. Pop built an aluminium awning over the verandah, and the frame for the awning and the supports were made from galvanised steel.

Originally there was a concrete slab underneath the house big enough for two cars to park, and beyond that it was unpaved dirt. There was an under-house garage with two tilted doors under the front verandah, and the concreted driveway was two-cars wide.

Police officers were often at the hospital where Maree worked, so back then the Nambour police knew all of us girls. This was not a good thing! Maree found out if you had done wrong before you even got home. Life was going sort of okay. I cannot remember seeing Dad at all after we moved into the new house.

Now, Maree was one for bed making. We were taught from an early age how to make a bed properly, and we had to do 'hospital corners' on our sheets. I do not know how many times I made that bloody rotten bed. If it was not done properly, Maree would rip the sheets, blankets, and pillow off the bed, "Do it again, and this time do it properly." I do not know how many times I did it, and it did not stop there. The cupboard drawers, oh me! Everything had to be folded up and put in the drawers neatly. How many times I re-tidied my drawers, (underpants, shirts, shorts, etc.,) all five of the mongrels!

It was about then I started to suffer from migraines, just as Dad did, so it's probably hereditary. I remember Maree wrapping me in wet sheets at the front door with a fan on me. As the years have gone by my migraines have become so severe that they are incurable, and the symptoms can only be managed with strong medication, hot and cold packs, over-the-counter painkillers, rubs and sprays, sitting in a shower for at least half an hour, and if none of those things work it's off to hospital for an injection.

SIX | 1974

The date was the 29th of June 1974, and at about 6 p.m. that day my life changed forever. I had no idea what was ahead of me! What followed was years of emotional abuse, physical abuse, mental abuse ... and more. I didn't yet know it, but from that night on my life was going to change for the worse.

We had a babysitter and housekeeper, called Eva, and she had a boyfriend named Mark. Each night Mark would come to the house to see Eva, and he would always talk to the three of us girls.

We had just sat down to our dinner when I heard a car pull into the driveway. Like most kids would, I jumped up and ran out to the front verandah. "Get back here and eat your tea!" screamed Maree. (Tea is what we called the evening meal.)

One of the police officers, who knew us well, was standing in the driveway beside his police vehicle. "Hi sir, what can I do for you?" I asked.

"Is your mum home, Donna? I need to talk to her," said the policeman.

And I replied, "You have come to tell Maree that Dad has been killed, haven't you?"

Now, just as I said that Maree appeared. "Hi, what can I do for you?"

The policeman answered, "Donna just told me what I came to tell you."

I turned around to face her, "Dad's been killed, that's what the policeman has come to tell you."

Maree asked, "Is that right?"

The policeman replied, "Yes, Maree, I am so sorry, but Ron has been killed in a car accident at Kureelpa, at the cutting. I need you to come down to the hospital and identify him."

"Okay, I will come down and do that," said Maree.

I said, "I want to come with you to see Dad!" Do you think Maree would let me go there?! It was going to be a bloody cold day in hell before she would let me go with her!

From that day to this, no one has been able to tell me how I already knew what the policeman had come to tell Maree. It just came out, not another word said. I do not know how I knew. But from that night forward my life was going to change in *all* ways — even ways that I could not imagine. The way family members and other people treated me, my own behaviour, my schooling, and my temper.

The policeman left, and by the time I got back inside everyone else had finished eating, but they were still sitting at the table. Maree screamed at me to sit down and finish my tea, then she got ready and went to the hospital to identify Dad.

Then something just snapped; dishes, etc., went flying and walls were hit. I was out of control! It took Mark slapping me across the face and holding me to calm me down. Then I was sobbing uncontrollably, "Dad, Dad, Dad," over and over again. All I wanted was my Dad, the man I loved regardless. I needed to see him.

It took a while for me to calm down ... but I have never truly *settled*. My temper flared far more often than it should have, and I frequently got into trouble. At that time, I just did not care.

My heart was broken, I did not want to talk to, or see, anyone else. I suppose I withdrew into myself. My Dad was gone, I would never see him again, never laugh with him, never get a hug or the top of my head rubbed in play, never do anything with him.

***

Because we had lived in Mapleton, Dad knew the road between Maleny and Nambour like the back of his hand, and particularly the part of the road at the cutting at Kureelpa where he was killed. He had driven that road in both cars and trucks, so I don't understand why he didn't steer around the corner. Instead the car drove straight — straight over the edge of the cutting. He was thrown out of the Valiant ute he was driving, and he landed on the rocky creek bottom below. Then the ute landed on top of him, crushing him.

The question no one has ever answered for me is, 'Why didn't Dad turn the corner?'

There are many questions that remain unanswered because people in my family, including extended family members, will not talk about Dad or his accident. Yet again, people think they know what is best for me and they will not be open and honest. To me they are not family.

Nambour Chronicle clipping reporting Dad's fatal car accident.
The damage to the roof and bonnet of the car is plain to see.

'A 36-year-old Nambour Man, Ronald Lawlor, was killed and two others injured when this utility overturned and landed in a creek on the Mapleton Road early on Saturday

night ... [the injured] were taken to Nambour General Hospital by ambulance. — Robinson Studios'
    [Names of the injured obscured for privacy reasons]

If only they stopped to think, they might understand that 'Donna deserves to know the truth about her dad's fatal car accident'. They should have realised the right thing to do was to tell me the truth, even if it was when I was older.

I found out that my cousin, who was an ambulance bearer, arrived at the scene of the accident. When he saw Dad's TNT shirt, he said, "That is Ron Lawlor!" He could not believe that Dad had been killed. It was tough for him to do his job that day, but that is what he had to do.

* * *

I had barely turned 12 years old at the end of May, so I was still only in grade seven. Maree refused to let us attend Dad's funeral, to say goodbye or to grieve for him. Maree arranged with our school that when the hearse carrying Dad — and all the other funeral cars — travelling from the church service to the Nambour Lawn Cemetery drove past the school, the three of us girls would go out and stand at the front fence.

I am still fucking pissed off about it, even writing about it all these years later upsets me. My Dad ... the tears flowed and flowed, but I felt like a spectacle standing at the front fence of the Nambour State School. I do not remember when my sisters went back to class, but I stood alone for a long time ... *left standing at the fence.*

Eventually, a teacher came and got me, but I do not remember returning to class. I know I did not stop crying for a long time, and kept saying, 'Dad'.

Put yourself in my place. He was the *one* person who no matter what happened, loved me, taught me things, made me laugh and, yes, disciplined me when I needed it, but he was my Dad — regardless.

I now know that my cousins, and other people, who saw us three girls left standing at the fence commented that we should have been at our father's funeral. They thought it looked awful, and they couldn't believe we were not allowed to attend the service. One of my cousins later apologised to me for not saying something at the time, but no one could stop Maree getting what she wanted.

People felt bad about it, but what could they do? Absolutely nothing! Maree did not like anything to do with Dad, and to her dying day it was the same. I felt that she was trying to shut Dad out of our lives. Like bloody hell — he is my Dad, in life and in death. With me she had no chance whatsoever.

Later in life I discovered I had a baby brother. Yes, I had a brother, but I was not allowed to know about him. It is unfair that the adults in my so-called family decided not to tell us girls about Keith Ronald. Why? Tracey was part of our life. A big part, and now she was the mum to our baby brother, who we were not allowed to know about or see. Oh, do not worry, Maree had seen him in hospital. To this day, I cannot forgive Maree for this.

I have never been able to find out any information on Keith's birth, but I believe my darling brother was born on the 4th of April 1974, which was about two months before Dad died.

Through information I found at the State Archives, I learned that when Dad died he and Maree had a pending court appearance in Townsville on the 4th of July for the divorce proceedings.

Oh yes, the information you find at the State Archives answers a lot of questions, but then there are a lot more questions that come from it. The evidence I read got my blood boiling! To this day I hate liars, and oh, my goodness talk about lies that were told about Dad and Tracey, by Maree.

To her dying day, Maree would not accept how I found out the facts. She wanted the information, and she wanted to stop the State Archives from letting people see the files. Ha, ha! I believe that yet again, she wanted to control everything and to cover up all the lies she had told. But this time she had met her worst nightmare. Me — Dad's shadow.

Oh, believe me, I found out things that were hard to accept, and I learned that she was the instigator of a lot of the trouble. Maree had led me to believe that we couldn't go out or be seen at pubs for a counter meal or at fairs, etc., because there was a court order in place, and we would be taken from her. For many, many years I believed all the lies and crap and bullshit told by Maree, but I found no documents to support those claims during my visit to the State Archives. So then I lost it — big time. In my opinion, she was a liar, a controller, and an abuser.

> A man died when he was pinned under his overturned car in shallow water in a creek bed off the Mapleton Road near Nambour at 5.30 p.m. on Saturday.
>
> He was Ronald Keith Lawlor, 36, married, of Nambour.

Another newspaper clipping about Dad's fatal car accident

'A man died when he was pinned under his overturned car in shallow water in a creek bed off the Mapleton Road near Nambour at 5.30 p.m. on Saturday.

He was Ronald Keith Lawlor, 36, married, of Nambour.'

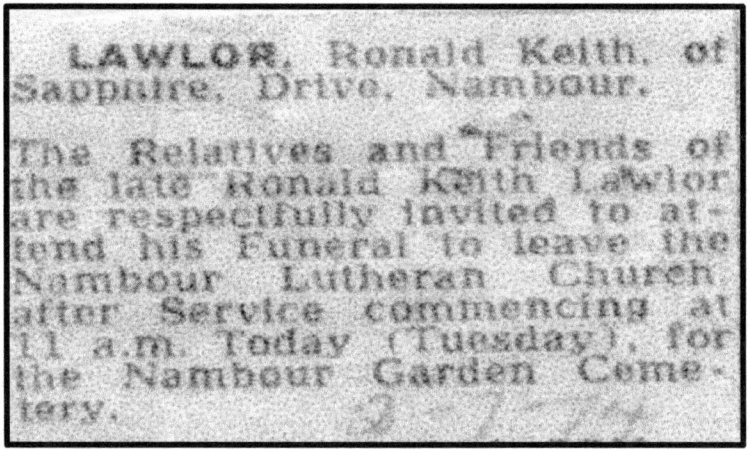

Funeral notice, sadly no mention of Dad's children, sister, mother, or father.

'**LAWLOR**, *Ronald Keith, of Sapphire Drive, Nambour.*

The Relatives and Friends of the late Ronald Keith Lawlor are respectfully invited to attend his Funeral to leave the Nambour Lutheran Church after Service commencing at 11 a.m. Today (Tuesday), for the Nambour Garden Cemetery.'

Source newspaper of above clippings unknown

SEVEN | 1974 to 1976

After Dad's passing, my life changed a lot. I was a person—*a child*—altered, damaged, and totally traumatised. I was becoming quiet, not wanting to do anything or talk to anyone, and at times I rebelled. Nothing, or no one, could make my life better.

At this time we started visiting Nana and Pop T, Dad's mum and stepfather, at their house out at Valdora. Now Pop is a story on his own! A funny bloke with a temper, I think he might have been Irish or something like that. He was also ex-Army, and now he was a hobby farmer. I loved Pop, and in his own way he loved and cared about me and my sisters.

Nana, oh what a woman! Nana had her own way of doing things, like everyone does, but she was so loving and caring. Nana should have been given an award for the **Best Grandmother**. With everything that I had going on, Nana was there to wipe away the tears, give me a hug, and, yes, tell me if I had done something wrong. Hey, at this time in my life I was no angel, but Nana's and Pop's was a place of love and happiness for me. They had a little dog called Tammy; Pop often called Tammy to him, and not in a polite way! But, even so, he loved that little dog.

Left Standing At The Fence

Oh, what a farm it was! Sometimes you couldn't find the gate to turn into it, because it was overgrown, and all you could see was the rough road up the hill. Remember, we were *'townies'*. When we finally reached the house, Maree would always joke, "When are going to fix the road up, Reg?"

Now about the house ... oh, to come from a new brick-built house with carpet and an inside *loo* (Australian slang for toilet) to an old-style farmhouse with the loo OUTSIDE! This was very strange to me.

I think Maree was the one who showed us the loo. She explained that when you went up to the loo, you must watch for snakes, like carpet snakes and red-bellied black snakes, to name a few. "You have to watch where you are walking for snakes." Holy shit! What was this place? But it was to get even worse.

"You go up the steps always looking, when you get to the door push it open with your foot, lean in, and have a look around, look up to the roof, if there's no snake in you go, and lift the lid and go to the toilet. You do not have to close the door, but everyone can see you, so be quick."

I can hear all of you laughing, but to a 12-year-old, who had never seen a snake, or an outdoor loo as gross as this one, it was terrifying! The loo was a little hut with a bench across the back, with a seat and lid in the middle. Even though we had an outside loo at Mapleton, this one was entirely different. Oh, my goodness, the stink was rank, foul, and disgusting!! Yuk, it made your stomach do somersaults.

Okay, it was in and out of the loo quickly, until ... One day, I needed to go to the loo, okay watch where I am walking, everything is clear. Check out the loo, all fine, now drop my pants, do what you must do, then suddenly, something made me look up. Well, I think I went through that bloody door, past the house, down the hill nearly all the way to the dam, with my undies around one ankle!

A big, fat, old carpet snake had come sliding through the roof of the loo onto one of the rafters. Well, now Pop was saying something, and swearing, while Nana was comforting me. Pop said that I had scared the snake. Okay, good on you Pop! It was a long time before I could go back into that loo, but I did because I loved it at Nana's and Pop's — much more than living with Maree.

Over the years, we often went out to the farm. One time, we arrived there and Pop was extending the back of the farmhouse. "Do not go out there, you might fall through the boards and hurt yourself," Nana warned all of us. Yaa right, Nana. Well, I didn't listen, I walked out on one of the boards, talking to Pop and not thinking. The next minute, I am through the floor, or that which is going to be the floor. Yes, I got some scratches, a bit of blood, and Nana — in her own way — told me I was in trouble. Being in trouble with Nana was nothing like being in trouble with Maree! All Pop could do was laugh, and it started me laughing too.

Anzac Day was a very special day for Pop. Nana spent days and days beforehand washing and ironing Pop's clothes, and polishing all of his medals. Come the morning, up early, wash and have breakfast, get dressed, wait for Pop. Now Pop being Pop, you could not rush him, BUT I could get him to move along.

*A proud Pop T on Anzac Day at Yandina, with me.
This is the only photo I have of him; I don't have any of Nana T.*

It was Pop, who taught me the importance of ANZAC Day, what it meant to people and the diggers. He was so proud in his suit, with that mongrel old, sticky, greasy hat on his head, and with his medals on his chest.

Now Anzac Day was a long day for Nana and the three of us girls. When the march was over, everyone moved over to the Yandina pub. As the day went on, Pop got a bit *happier* than normal, and I do not know how we got home safely. Well, back in the 1970s, drink driving wasn't talked about, it wasn't even a *thing*. Legless, in the little red Mazda, off we go, no Pop, backwards! Okay, now forwards! Nana could not drive, but she helped Pop with everything all the way home. Many a time we stayed in the wrong gear, and the little red Mazda car was screaming, but you could not hear it over Pop's singing. When Pop got drunk he sang, oh me, and you did not escape him either.

In no way am I saying Pop was a violent drunk at all. Far from it. Yes, he liked to have a drink now and then. Nine times out of ten he would fall asleep snoring. Back then men drank and drove. Remember, my pop was a veteran, I am so thankful for the sacrifice he made for my freedom.

To this day I do not know how on earth we got home in one piece! And not long after we got home Pop would go to sleep, usually with a beer in his hand. Peace at last, Nana got us out of our good clothes, and it was always, "Do not go and wake Pop up!"

Left Standing At The Fence

Every time I woke Pop up he would wake up saying "Okay girl, be there rightly," whether it was for a 'cuppa and pikelets' or just for a cuppa. Now Nana was a great cook. Oh, how we were spoilt, but always in a good way. Cakes and slices, cordial, frozen ice blocks, but never too much.

I remember standing up in the backyard looking over towards the house cleaning my teeth, with a glass of water. Nana always insisted that we cleaned our teeth twice a day. "If you do not clean your teeth you are going to be like me — gummy." And with that she would pull her top and bottom teeth out of her mouth. We would laugh and laugh!

Pop loved this one special dish for breakfast, but not every day. Nana cooked it, and she taught me — or tried to. Bacon fried until crispy; then liver — skinned, sliced into slabs: not too thick and not too thin. Rolled in egg, then into breadcrumbs, fried in a hot pan. Oh, cannot wait. Now the gravy ... you could not have liver and bacon without the gravy. Onion cut up small, and the special ingredients: Vegemite and coffee essence.

Now, many people don't like liver, okay that is fine, but this was *so* delicious, it was always back for more, and do not forget a slice of bread to wipe up the gravy. I have tried and tried to make it the same way, but without success. I always looked forward to going to Nana's and Pop's, because I knew we would get liver and bacon. Yummy!

At Nana's and Pop's, the mailman would come, and with him would be the newspaper and bread. We would stand out on the verandah and watch for him. Nana knew approximately the time he would come each day.

"Nana, the mailman is here," we would tell her.

With that, we would go way down the hill to the mailbox, which was not a box but a little shed. Of course, watch out for snakes! Now sometimes we would get there before the mailman, and he would always have a talk with Nana and us.

Get the mail, etc., and back up the hill. The bread was a high-top loaf and Nana always cut it just right, and it was so soft, and so good to eat. We were not allowed to disturb Pop because he was reading the papers.

Now, when Pop did his temper, it was 'watch out and get ready to duck'. Pop never ever lost his temper to any of us girls or to Nana. It was only at tractors that refused to work or if he was building something. On this particular day, Pop was working on the old tractor and something happened, well, the swear words were coming thick, fast, and loud! And next thing, a tool of some sort was flying through the air towards the dam, just like nearly every other tool that was thrown. It makes me laugh today remembering Pop 'doing his block', and the tool flying through the air. Something would go wrong and away Pop would go, "Rotten, bloody, stupid, metal, piece of junk!" With that, a hammer or some tool would go flying, and nine times out of ten, land in the dam. It was said that when they drained the dam, the bottom was full of tools.

Nana always went off at Pop for going mad on things and swearing when we were around, "Reg, the girls — watch your language!" Pop did ... for a while.

I cannot remember him ever going to the dam and getting a tool out from it, he would just go out and buy a new one. I suppose that is where I got it from — when something happens usually a tool or something goes flying. The worst part is, I have to go and pick the rotten, friggin', mongrel thing up!

When it was cane season and we were at Nana's and Pop's, we would stand out on the verandah of a night, with the mosquitoes, and we would watch all the cane fires. It was a beautiful sight. Nana's and Pop's house was on the side of a mountain and you could see for miles. Back then, the cane trains ran alongside Valdora Road, so the drivers all knew Pop and Nana, and somehow, they knew us by name too.

Nana and Pop got on in years and the farm got too much for them, particularly for Nana. So, they sold the farm and bought a nice house right next door to the Yandina pub. So, the next time I saw Nana and Pop they were in the new house with a loo inside. I could not believe it, great!

The high-set house was built-in underneath and it also had vegetable gardens. Nana and Pop grew some of the vegetables for the pub's kitchen, and those gardens were extended many times. There was a short, white fence along the front of the property, with gates on the driveway.

"Close the gates, or the dog will get out!" Nana would yell when you arrived.

Life was much the same in Yandina for Nana and Pop. Pop still had his afternoon sleep and Nana ruled the house. Oh, how she ruled it ... but in a good and caring way.

Nana had her own religious beliefs, and she hated the people who came to the door and tried to talk religion to her. Even out on the farm, I had seen grown men running down the hill from Nana—but in town, oh, my goodness!

One day there was a knock at the door. Pop got the door, the next minute the door shut and Pop yelled, "Your friends are at the door!" Well, we knew what that meant. To the front door with Nana, "What do you bloody want? I have a cake cooking!"

"We would like to talk to you about God."

"I'm not interested, now get out of here before I put the dog on you."

I have seen many a grown man try to take on Nana and lose. Tammy, the dog, was more noise than anything else. When Nana had finished saying her bit the front door was in motion. That door got slammed so hard I do not know how the glass did not break.

"Nana, they're not going," we would yell out, or there would be another knock on the door.

"Tammy, come here. What are you still doing here? I told you to go. Tammy, put them out!"

It was funny for a child to see these two men going down the stairs, two and three at a time, with Tammy on their heels. Often, they would just jump the front fence, but one got their pants leg caught on the spike of the gate or the fence, and landed face-first on the driveway.

"Tammy, come back here! Don't you two ever come back!"

They came back, not them but others, and they kept coming. I suppose Nana slamming that door is probably where I picked up slamming doors. All I can say is I had a good teacher.

Sadly, we did not see as much of Nana and Pop after they moved to Yandina. Then after a while we didn't see Nana and Pop at all. Why? Maree!! Yet again she caused hurt by taking away people who I loved. And they loved me so much!

Nana and Pop T sold the house some years later and moved to Miriam Vale. I cannot remember seeing them again until I was an adult.

Now, looking back with a bit of understanding, going out to Nana's and Pop's gave me a release from all Maree was doing to me. Time at Nana's and Pop's was filled with love ... love I didn't get at home. I didn't realise back then how special the times with them were. All *my* memories of my time with Nana and Pop are still so special to me.

EIGHT | 1976

We were raised in a religious home from the time we came back from Townsville, and even to when we moved the **'family'** home. Every Sunday it was get up, have breakfast, get dressed, and then it was down to Maroochydore to the Lutheran church. Those wooden pews were uncomfortable for a child to sit on.

Christmas 1976, Nana, Maree, and the three of us girls had been to church. We got to Nana's home and started getting lunch organised when the phone rang. Now Pop had been sick for a while, and was in hospital. Maree answered the phone and then spoke to Nana. I do not remember exactly what followed, but again things changed. My darling Pop had passed away. I can't remember the last time I saw him before he died. Of course, Maree didn't allow us to go to Pop's funeral, so now there was another person I loved who I did not get to say goodbye to. All I have is a special memory of seeing Nana's house bursting with bouquets of flowers and other floral tributes, all paying respect to my Pop.

* * *

Pop's cousins lived on a farm at Toogoolawah. The farm was on the Brisbane River, and Maree and the three of us and Nana would visit there.

Oh, how I hated it! But we **had** to go, we were forced to go, never given a choice whether we wanted to go or not!

They had a dairy, grew hay, and harvested it. They grew watermelons, oh, not like you get in the shops now, but these melons, were long, light green ones that tasted *so* sweet you wanted more. I think the other variety they grew were called Port melons, they were a big, round, dark green melon and tasted nothing like watermelons taste today. You could smell how sweet they were.

They had many farm implements, and one day everyone was running over to the shed. Uncle with the shotgun, others with rakes, etc., and the dogs were barking loudly. We were told to stay back out of the road but, of course, a child is interested. A snake was in the grain-seeder. A big, red-bellied black snake! Somehow it came out of the grain-seeder, but it did not live long!

There was a white horse at the farm, it was old and grumpy, and only Uncle could go near it.

They had a big farmhouse built high off the ground, with many steps to go up to it. Everything was upstairs, and underneath the house were chairs and a table to sit at, out of the heat.

Left Standing At The Fence

There was a cousin who I did not like at all, and every time we went over he was there. I remember this one time in particular: I had brought a book with me to read, I was lying in one of the chairs out of the heat, and he came downstairs. The next minute he tried to lie on top of me and kiss me.

I do not remember how I got away from him, but I went upstairs and told Maree, only to be told, "He is only trying to give you a kiss. Go back downstairs and be quiet!" This happened on more than one occasion, and I **hated** going to the farm. Why he was not stopped, I do not know. Why did someone not say something? I do not know to this day.

The farm was on the Brisbane River so when it was hot, we would all go down to the river for a swim, and the cousins would catch some fish as well.

I was frightened at first, the water was dark and then you would feel something around your legs. But I got used to the water, and in the end I loved it. I would swim out to my cousin in the middle of the river, and then from the bank, "Get back in here!" Maree would yell. I was with my cousin who could swim and who had been swimming in the river — I do not know how many times — but I had to stay in water to my knees.

As the years went on, I was able to stay upstairs and listen to the radio program, *Bellbird*, in the afternoon. You were **not** allowed to speak while the show was on. As time went on we went over more and more, and I still dreaded going there. It was boring, hot, and lonely. The cousin had two adult children, but they never did anything with us that I can remember.

* * *

The police officer who we stayed with in Townsville moved to Nambour to start the Police Citizens Youth Club there. Maree enrolled us in gymnastics, but it was not for me. Swimming, well, I took to that like a duck to water! I was not a thin child, a bit chubby, but I could still fit into a one-piece swimsuit.

We had swimming lessons, and then each Thursday night (I think) was competition night. No matter what I did, for some reason, I came last in every race except for backstroke. I cannot remember how many times my arm smacked hard into the wall.

When I was swimming up and down the pool I thought about Dad, but then out of nowhere Maree's booming voice would be yelling at me. Back to reality! I swam for about four or five years. It never mattered that I did not become a champion swimmer, I loved doing it, and it was an escape.

To raise funds, the Police Citizens Youth Club put on the play *Dimboola*, with a meal. *Okay, I'm going to give it a go*, I thought, so I put my name down for an acting role. This would be great, something I can do. Bugger me dead, Maree put her name down too!

Now, if you do not know the play it is about a just-married couple, the bride is heavily pregnant, and the groom is a little slow. The show is set during the wedding reception and all sorts of antics go on there. The mother-of-the-bride chases people over and under tables, and yells out throughout the play.

So, when it came to casting, what part did I get? The bride! What part did Maree get? The mother-of-the-bride! Great, but the biggest insult was I had to wear *her* bloody wedding dress, which was made of heavy, hot Ironbark satin.

I loved the play. It was fun, but it called for hugs and kisses from groom to bride. Well, as you can guess that did not go over too well, I got the *devil stare* over the glasses from Maree. Then on the last night of the play, oh, what a night it was! The play went well, and the breakup party was great, until Maree caught me on the verandah kissing the groom. Oh, I paid a price, but to be yelled at in front of a large room full of local councillors and businessmen was too much. I felt hurt, I was a spectacle, and no good.

I took off. I had changed out of her bloody wedding dress, tears were flowing down my face, and I walked. I just wanted my Dad. She had the police looking for me, of course. But I was the one who paid the price, "How dare you make a fool of me in front of businessmen and people from the club!" Maree screamed.

I never put my name down for another thing. I now knew what humiliation was, and I did not like it one bit.

From 1975 to 1978 I attended Nambour High School. School was not a happy place for me. I got bullied in high school by the same children who had bullied me in state school. And now there were others who bullied me too. I could not escape the name they called me constantly, *'Lawlor the Crawler'*.

I was bullied, left by myself, and made fun of at sport — different groups of kids picked on me. When I complained to Maree, nothing was done. The only time she did try to do something was when the headmistress at the high school put me on rubbish duty during 'big lunch' for something I did not do. Maree came to the school, and everyone heard her, which made my life worse! Kids can be so damn cruel.

I never fitted in at school the whole time I was there. When I did misbehave, somehow, Maree knew about it before I got home. Because the police knew who I was, I could not do a thing wrong.

There was a bloke I was spending time with after school, and the local policeman caught me. Shit, here goes! Well, it turned out the bloke was on a bet to go out with me. When I found out, I lost it.

He got a mouthful out of me, and then I discovered who had put on the bet — one of the policeman's sons! I had swimming that afternoon and I knew he would be there at the club. I did not hold back, he got told off, and that included some Aussie slang and swearwords, plus and open hand across the face.

Because of the loudness of my voice, and the swearing—OH, IT WAS PRETTY DIRTY SWEARING—his dad came out of the office to see what was going on. As I was walking away his dad stopped me, and asked me what had happened. He was not happy with what I told him, and he said sorry to me. Sorry to *me*, was not up to him, but his son. The bloke paid a price for it, though, because I hardly spoke to him again.

Now, at this time Maree was extending the back of the house. Right along the back of the house, to make a new dining room/kitchen, back door and storage area, and a new bedroom.

I wanted the new bedroom. No, you have yours! So, my little sister got the new room. I would have been okay with that, except now there was a big window between our rooms. Now, as you can imagine there were fights over the window being open or closed. I wanted it open because in summer my room was *so* hot. I only had one small window in my room, and it was where the summer sun beat down—blaring hot. After all the fighting over the room and the window, I stayed in my room for a few more years.

* * *

When I would get into trouble from Maree it was with yelling, finger pointing, smacking with a hand or a leather belt, ear-pulling, and spitting in the face.

My punishment would often consist of me walking to and from school in grades nine, ten and eleven. That didn't worry me because the bus was hell! Two boys lived in my area and they always took the bus. They made so much fun of me that I often ended up in tears. Because of them, I walked more times than I caught the bus.

In grade ten, I took refuge in the library during breaks. I enjoyed the peace and quiet.

From about grade nine onwards I worked weekends at the shop that had been Nana's and Pop's. I enjoyed it, and the new owners, Judy and Col, were fantastic. They were like loving parents — they had three boys, who I babysat sometimes — they taught me so much: how to talk to a customer, how to use a cash register, and how to use a meat slicer, etc. I was only paid a small wage, but at least now I was earning my own money and was able to buy my own things.

One day I had to refill the drink fridge. Back then *Coca-Cola* ® (coke) came in glass bottles, and a large bottle of coke slipped from my hands and exploded on the concrete floor. The owners asked if I was alright, and I answered yes ... but I was **not** okay.

I did not realise straight away that I had been injured. I had a deep cut, about five centimetres long, just above the front of my ankle. Judy was quick, she put a clean tea towel on my ankle and took me down to the hospital. Oh no, here goes! Maree was at work and had already been called.

When I arrived at the hospital, they took me into the small operation room in Emergency. Next thing, the doors flew open and in stormed Maree, even though I had already been attended to. Here comes a storm — category five *Cyclone Maree*! Why? I had asked to be allowed to shave my legs because the hairs on my legs were long and black, and I was getting bullied about it at school.

Well, one look and that was it. "I told you that you were **not** allowed to shave your legs. Wait until I get home, I will deal with you then. I have had enough of you not listening!"

I had been saving all my money from working at the shop, and I had just bought a pair of jeans and a new pair of blue Adidas shoes. When Maree looked at the wound, she wanted to cut off the jeans and my shoes. "Like bloody hell, I paid for these because you would not buy them for me. Go to hell, you are not cutting these jeans!" I screamed at her. I told her to leave me alone, at the same time as I was kicking her in the arm. A doctor and nurses were looking after me already, and I didn't need her barging in and trying to take control.

I won against Maree that time, but it was one of only very few occasions when I did.

"This is going to need stitches," Maree said.

"Not on your bloody nelly!" I screamed.

"Just strap it together and put a bandage around it, and I am out of here," I said.

Maree said that I had to go home and put my leg up. No, I had part of a shift left to work, so yes, I did go back to work. Judy was great, after we left the hospital I cried and cried, "Why does she treat me so badly? Why does she hurt me and hate me? I can't do anything right. I'm frightened about what is going to happen tonight." Judy wiped the tears away and said I could rest up at their place. Their home was the back shed turned into a house. "No, I've got a shift to finish, and Col is by himself."

However, that night, I remember being told off and yelled at—Maree made me feel like I was nothing but trouble. But the worst thing was, when I said something the belt came out. Yes, I wore that leather belt around my bottom and legs again.

As I grew up the belt stopped hurting, I do not know whether it was because I could handle the pain better or if I had just had enough. But when Maree hit me for the last time with the belt ... well let's just say a wall got a fist through it and all I did was laugh. Now, that just made Maree madder than a Brahman bull. Yep, I was mad too. Had enough. That was not the only wall that had my fist through it. A few even got my foot.

So now my new discipline from Maree was to grab the top of my ear, twist it, and pull me up on to my tippy toes. Believe you me, that mongrel bloody thing hurt when it was done for a while, and especially if it was only the edge she had! Try it, and you will see it hurts!

At that time I was hurting deeply, and no one understood or cared that I was a mess, or *why* I was a mess. I felt alone, unwanted, unloved, I was trouble and a problem ... all I wanted was my Dad.

NINE | 1977

Of course Maree continued to work ... and work ... and work ... and work.

When I got to an age, I must have been about 15, I would make Maree's gin and squash. Remember, I said I was rebelling. Well, make it a bit stronger, have a good drink, and then take it out to Maree. One summer afternoon, I made the drinks and had some myself, but evidently, I had too much.

Now, I don't remember anything about what took place next, but apparently this did happen. The house was built high off the ground so the drop from the verandah to the concrete driveway was a long drop. The verandah railing was only about five centimetres wide, but no problem, I walked along that verandah railing. Meanwhile, Maree was holding her breath, and when I finally stepped down I was put straight to bed. Oh hell, the next morning my head throbbed — welcome to a hangover! Of course, I got into trouble with the usual ear-pull and mouthful. And I was never allowed to make Maree's drinks again!!

Of all the teenagers around my age who lived near me, there was one person who became my friend — Kath M. We were the terrible twins in crime! Kath M had a great mum, and she was allowed to go to friend's places, roller-skating, and parties. Not me! If I went to Kath M's on a school afternoon, I had to be home by 4.30 p.m. or 5.00 p.m. I got better at running between our homes when the clock was nearly at 5.00 p.m., but to make things worse, you could see Kath M's place, and the way I came home, from our front verandah. So, no escaping the clock!

Kath M's mum was so nice to me when I was at their home, and I became jealous. Jealous because her mum treated her with love and cared about her. She was a real mum, just like I wanted so much.

Now, Kath M's house had a back verandah, and under it her family had a big cage where they had a white cockatoo. I don't know if Kath M's Mum knew, but Kath M would smoke at the back of the cage. One day her mum caught me, Kath M, and another friend smoking. It was the first time I had smoked a full cigarette. Kath M's mum was angry with us and she said that there would be no more smoking at her place, and that I had better go home.

Well, Maree was a smoker, so I did not think she would suspect anything. Wrong!! She smelt it, and I got asked one hundred questions. Then I got the ear-pull, as I called it. I did have the occasional smoke after that, and even though I knew it was wrong, I would occasionally take one or two cigarettes from Maree's packet.

I spent a lot of time with Kath M over the years, and when I was at her house I could listen to the music of our generation: ABBA and Bay City Rollers to mention a couple. It was great. Oh, how I wanted to have my own music. Not on, Maree said, "That music is bad, and it won't be in my house."

As the years went on the music did come into the house — plus more. She had *her* music, which drove me to go under the house or on a pushbike ride. Her music was old country, Slim Dusty, gospel, and that's just a start. Yes, I like some of Slim Dusty's music, and old country, but hey, I was a teenager and I wanted to listen to teenager's music.

There were times I got in trouble because of my friendship with Kath M. Unfortunately, Kath M and I eventually lost contact, but I remember how I wish I'd had her life. Her mum was great. She answered the questions that a mother should have. When we lived at Nana's and Pop's, and I was in primary school, the high school headmistress came over to talk to all the girls about *female things*! I sat there like a stunned mullet — I had not heard of any of it.

When I got home I asked Maree about it. I was given a midwifery textbook and told to read a certain chapter. It frightened the hell out of me! I did not understand a bit of it. Fortunately, Kath M's mum was patient enough to explain those things to me.

I was still rebelling, and my mouth continued to get me into trouble, so I landed in hot water again. But this time it was worse. No seeing Kath M again, and no going for bike rides. School, work, and home—that was my new world. That was my punishment.

I could not win, no matter what I did or said I ended up in trouble.

Throughout my younger years, and right up until I left home, I was not allowed to go to any parties. Yep, you got it, not a one. Maree said it was something to do with a 'court order and children's services'. What a joke. Through my research, I learned there were **no** fucking court orders or notifications from children's services to where we, us girls, could go or what we could not do. I will go into that later in more depth. All it was, again, was Maree trying to be in control.

All those years I believed what Maree said. So, I never had the enjoyment of going to any parties and spending time with people socially. I never learned how to talk to other people or how to communicate with them. The only parties we went to were with our cousins or other family members. Definitely not children's parties or teenager's parties.

I remember my birthday presents and Christmas presents usually were underwear or school stuff. It was only later in life that I started to get gifts that I *wanted*, rather than just things I *needed*.

* * *

Left Standing At The Fence

My friend, Mr L, was a 2nd black dan in karate and he had taught me a bit of it. So, he got to know me, my likes, my dislikes, my favourite foods — everything. For a while we had an above-ground pool. We lived in it. One day when Mr L was visiting us he picked me up and tried to throw me in the pool. Somehow I got out of his hold and we started rumbling, and the next thing he was kicked in the jaw and was flying through the air, thanks to my karate moves.

He missed the clothes hoist by about an inch. Maree was in the kitchen and saw *all* of it. Mr L hit the ground and I was right there. I felt so bad. Tears were flowing down my face; I had hurt Mr L! I kept asking him if he was okay. He said he was, but he had to go home that night.

He came back to see us a couple of weeks later and he told me he would not be teaching me any more karate. Why? Well, my kick had cracked his jaw. Not badly, but cracked, nonetheless. I felt awful I had hurt him. I never meant it.

Maree had made us all long dresses to wear to the Kenilworth Rodeo Ball. Where she went, we had to go. Boring! She would be talking to adults all night and there would be nothing for us kids to do. The music and the dancing at the ball was so old-fashioned!!

Pop, Maree's Dad, had made us a pool table, complete with snooker balls. One day, I was in a bad mood — with the temper to match — and for some reason I hit someone. And broke the pool cue in half across their back! I never played pool on that table again.

See, that Irish/Welsh/German temper is a bad one!

TEN | 1977 to 1981

As the years went on I still rebelled, and my discipline was still the 'ear-pull'.

No matter what I did, nothing was right. Still!

In about 1977 or thereabouts, Eve left, and we got another babysitter/housekeeper. I think there were a couple of them. Maree kept working and I cannot recall any happy times. I still did my swimming and went to school. I finished grade 10 with a grade of C's, got a D for shorthand.

"You should have studied more, you should have practiced more, why are you always causing problems?"

I did not care. What was I going to do next year? I took a grade 11 one-year course. Later that year I got a job. Of course, my employers were friends of Maree. I liked the job at the café. It was enjoyable. I was learning something, and I got along with the woman who owned the business.

But then I was set up—framed!—by another person, and in the end I lost my job. What was I going to do? I looked for work in the usual places and I found an advertisement for a dairy hand. I applied for the job and got it.

At last, I am out of home. I can now be me! You bet I can now be ME.

I started working on a dairy farm at Kenilworth. Hmm ... the house was not flash, but I thought it was great in other ways. I was welcomed in, and no one judged me, no one looked me up and down. I was me, and it felt good. There was another lady working there already and she was leaving soon to get married. Oh, Susan and I had such a ball. I had my first taste of rum, and yes, I coughed like a steam train going up a hill at first, but then I got the taste for it. Rum! Yum! More please, love my rum!

One morning at breakfast—*after* milking the cows and putting them out to pasture—Susan and I were told that a new person would be arriving tomorrow morning. As this person was a male, we were asked to set up the other room for him. We were not told anything about him so, of course, we started guessing.

Then the next morning while we were milking, Susan said to me, "I bet he is a nerd with glasses, and a smart ass who has never worked on a farm."

I said, "No, long haired, young, rides a motorbike, worked on dairy farms before." Okay, so what are we going to bet on this?

We both thought about it, and I came up with, "If he is what you say, I owe *you* two double-rums, but if he is what I say, you owe *me* two double-rums." Okay, we agreed. Now, I had already seen the motorbike arrive at the house, so I could not get down there quickly enough!

We still had to finish milking, so my mind turned back to that. When the milking was finished, this was the first and only time we had run from the dairy to the house. I got the two double-rums that night in the Kenilworth pub!

His name was Tony, he rode a motor bike, he had long hair.

* * *

I loved it on the dairy farm at Kenilworth. The family I worked for also had a stud farm at Obi Obi. We were having breakfast one morning when Frank, the boss, came in.

"Okay, Donna, I want you to pack your gear after breakfast, you are going to the stud farm to work."

Great! I did not know anyone at the stud farm, I would be the only worker there, *and* I was moving away when I was just getting to know Tony.

That night Frank took me over to the stud farm. Tony and I had agreed to keep in touch.

Now Frank's brother, Jock, and his sister, Dorothy, ran the stud farm. The farmhouse was basic, but it was home for Jock and Dorothy, and they were great people.

I woke up the next morning and went out to see the farm. The daily routine was: wake, cuppa, get cows, milking etc., and go back to the house for breakfast. After breakfast, there were different jobs that needed to be done.

I loved this farm. It was great, and Jock taught me a lot. Dorothy was a great lady, sometimes she could be short with me, but overall she was a good woman.

This farm was different to Frank's: the dairy was different, and the cows were a different breed here — purebred Australian Illawarra Shorthorn. They were beautiful cows, and I had to learn their names. There were many to learn.

For a bath on the farm, you had to carry a tin of hot water from the dairy down to the house. That tin of water used to get damn heavy after a while!

* * *

It was my 17th birthday, and it didn't get off to a good start.

I woke up full of energy and was looking forward to the day. I was enjoying my morning cup of tea, but it suddenly went flying all over the table ... What the hell was going on here?!

Similar incidents continued to happen, but I didn't go to the doctor because I had to work. I had no idea what was wrong and how sick I really was!

Of course, Dorothy got mad about my little accidents, but Jock was caring. I tried to ignore that something was not right with me because I wanted to work and learn, and I learnt a lot: mustering, helping with calving, searching for calves lost in long grass, and cleaning all the show gear.

I enjoyed the long walks looking for cows and their calves. I would get impatient with calves walking 'home', to the point I would put them on my shoulders and walk a mile or two back to the dairy. I am paying a price for that now!

Tony and I stayed in touch. He wanted to take me out, but I did not have a bike helmet. My friend, Bob, lived at Conondale, and he brought a helmet over one weekend for me to borrow. Working on the farm, we would work so many days and then get some time off. So Tony and I spoke to Frank and Jock, and it was agreed we could have our days off at the same time.

Now I had the helmet I could go with Tony on the bike—something I had never done. I loved the bike, but, of course, Maree did not! The first night we pulled up at Maree's house, oh my goodness, away she went.

"Who is that?! What are you doing on a bike?! You are going to kill yourself!"

Blah, blah, blah!

I did not listen, and I did not care. Naturally, we did not call in and see Maree much after that, but we did spend a lot of time on the bike! Many times getting home in the early morning, and no sleep—just straight to work.

Life at the stud farm was okay. I got into trouble for staying out late and coming back in the early mornings. Of course, Maree had phoned Jock and spoken to him about me going out, so in a way I was grounded.

Tony and I continued to spend a lot of time together and we formed a serious relationship. We went everywhere on the bike. We had fun, I showed Tony various parts of the Coast and we even met his brother and his family.

We arranged to go to Brisbane one weekend. Tony was to pick me up by a certain time for us to catch the train. That time came and went. I finally got hold of Susan at Frank's farm and she told me that Tony had unfortunately had a bike accident. He was okay, but we would not be going away for the weekend. I got Jock to take me over to the dairy farm.

Oh, Tony had done well! He had a cut on the hand that his glove had stayed on, and a cut on his foot that the boot had stayed on. But his back had been badly hurt. The whole of his back was covered in 'gravel rash', skin off, and the blood was starting to stop. I managed to get the gravel out of Tony's wounds, but we needed to put something on them to stop the bleeding and protect his skin.

Now, remember Maree hadn't taught me any first aid. The only thing we had was Susan's Vaseline Intensive Care Lotion. We started to put it on very gently when Tony let out a scream. The lotion was stinging his back, so we stopped that, and very gently washed his back to get it off.

I had not wanted to, but I had to ring Maree.

I told her what had happened and asked what to do. No, I did not have any of the items she mentioned. She was going to bring over the medications and dressings we needed. Oh, here we go, now we are going to get the third degree! Thank goodness we had a bottle of rum and a bottle of Southern Comfort. Maree arrived, complaining that she'd had to drive the Obi Obi range at night. She had a look at Tony's wounds and put mercurochrome on them. Boy, did that stuff stain!

The next day Frank took us down to where the accident happened. You could not see the bike from the road. The cause of the accident? Three heifers had been on the road. One had to be put down, that was the one that had the bike go up its rear end!

After the accident, the handlebars of the bike were in a higher position than before, and being that there was no headlight, a Dolphin torch (Eveready® Dolphin™) was strapped on as a substitute headlight.

In winter, it was freezing on the bike, so after a time Tony finally got a car. He had no licence for a car, but he drove anyway. We decided to go for a trip to see his aunt. It was great meeting his aunt and her children. We were coming back from Alstonville, driving down the range and he clipped a car. Now, this was in New South Wales, but everyone—and I mean everyone!—knew about the car accident before we got back to Kenilworth in Queensland. As time went on, he did get his licence, but for some reason cattle did not like his car! Another time, Tony was driving on the main road into Kenilworth, and there were calves out on the road. Unfortunately he hit one. This car must be bad luck!

Then, in September 1979, I injured my back on the farm. I cannot remember who took me to my doctor in Nambour, but I never returned to work on the farm.

Maree was on a holiday over in Western Australia when I hurt my back. "Tony is not to stay at the house while I am not there," all the way from bloody Western Australia. Oh my God, I cannot do anything! He was staying with me of a night and working all day.

It is strange looking back at this, because at that time Mr L would visit me too. It was very confusing. Here I loved Tony, but I also loved Mr L. In the end, my heart went with Tony. Maree came home to find that Tony had stayed with me, and that he had been caring for me while she had been away. To say she was *not* happy would be an understatement! As time went on, we went for a holiday, and came back.

Left Standing At The Fence

It was December 1979 when I was finally diagnosed with epilepsy. I did not understand what epilepsy was, and I knew nothing about it other than I had to take medication for it. So, about the beginning of December, I had not taken my tablets for about three days, and that morning I threw a Grand Mal seizure. My bed was about thirty centimetres from the wall in my bedroom, and I fell down into that gap. Maree was home, and she tried to pull me up. It was stupid for a nurse to do that. It's silly, I remember punching and kicking, and connecting a few times, but other than that, I was dazed and sleepy.

Maree called the ambulance and I was taken to hospital, and I do not remember how long I stayed there. I hadn't known that I should not stop taking the tablets for my epilepsy, **and** that I would have to take them for the rest of my life. No one had explained anything about epilepsy to me.

* * *

The boss from the Kenilworth dairy farm tracked Tony down and he started working back there. By this time we lived in a unit in Cooroy, and I did some casual work at the Nambour Hospital. Prior to Christmas Tony and I had thrown around talk of marrying. On Christmas Day 1980, I asked him to marry me, and it was not a leap year either. He said yes! Now there was no engagement ring—that did not come until 1990—

but we announced our engagement during Christmas lunch at Maree's.

In most families, there is joy and congratulations, pats on the back and a beer for the bloke. Not for us. We chose the 25th of July 1981 as our wedding date, which would be ten days after Nana's birthday on the 15th of July. Tony kept working on the farm, and on the 25th of July 1981, we got married.

A woman looks forward to organising her wedding. I looked at all the books and window-shopped, but to no avail. With Maree it was like this, "You are having ***this!***" Okay, we did not have a lot of money and we were very grateful to Maree for paying for the wedding, and for her help. But hey, the only thing I had control of was that I was not walking up the aisle to Tony with Maree. I asked a neighbour who was close to me, and he did me the honour of walking me up the aisle and giving me away.

When it came to the dress, it was made to Maree's instructions, and I got no say on what it was going to be. I can remember feeling like a puppet on my wedding day. The only clear memory I have is of the ceremony and that we messed up the kiss—which brought laughter from our (or rather, Maree's) guests.

Every woman wants her wedding to be special. It is supposed to be the only one, right? Yes, ours was great, but Maree *again* told me what to wear, what to have, whom to invite ... and then the time the reception would finish! Why? Because she planned a birthday party for Nana straight *after* the reception. Now remember, Nana's birthday had been on the 15th of July, ten days before our wedding. So now our wedding reception was rushed to accommodate Nana's birthday party. Sadly, I do not even remember the wedding reception or going to Nana's birthday party because it was a blur.

Even on our honeymoon we had to do a run-around to exchange wedding gifts. After the honeymoon was over it was back to work for Tony, and sometime after that we moved into a house on the farm.

Sitting on Tony's motorbike, taken after his accident

*In Maree's choice of a wedding dress.
Beautiful bouquet of orchids made by Nana.*

ELEVEN | 1983 to 1991

Tony and I had our first child, Colleen Lee, in March 1983 at Nambour Hospital. Sister Polly — the maternity wing sister who had delivered me — helped me through two days of labour, to deliver my baby. Dr P was my GP, and he was also my obstetrician. He was great; he was funny, he was understanding, and he would be there any minute of the day.

I was a week overdue, when on Saturday afternoon we had a car accident. On Sunday I went into quiet labour, and on Monday afternoon Colleen was born. Of course, Maree came in at various times during the labour. Sister Polly retired from nursing the week Colleen was born. I'd had no epilepsy tablets for the two days I was in labour, so what happened on Tuesday morning? A seizure — great! Oh well.

It then came time for Colleen to be christened. Again, Maree had to be involved. Christ can't I do anything on my own or with Tony? It was evident that Maree had to be in control, even when I was a married woman with a child.

So, what did Maree do? She turned Colleen's christening into my 21st birthday party. I did not enjoy it, and I do not remember much of it.

In late 1983 Tony, Colleen, and I moved to Goondiwindi, known by locals as 'Gundy'. The farmhouse was a three-quarter of an hour drive from Gundy.

One day Maree phoned me to say that Pop T had died. No information, just that he had died. No information on the funeral arrangements, etc. Nothing! Another person gone. He was the third family member to die that I did not get to say goodbye to. At least he got to see Colleen and hold her. So, I remember him the way he was: funny, loving, caring ... just Pop.

After a time, we moved to Glenmorgan. Life was going okay, and Tony was working on a mixed farming station. We went kangaroo shooting, fishing, and for picnics at the dam. No one was around to tell me what to do, or to try to control me — at the age of 21 or older.

Things were going along okay until ... one day in late September or early October 1985, we were on our way home from shopping in Dalby when we called in to see the GP in Tara to get the results of an x-ray Tony had previously. We did not think everything would be turned upside down so quickly.

Tony had to go to Toowoomba Hospital straight away to have one of his kidneys removed. Well, things did not go as planned. He nearly died a few times. I was four months pregnant with our second child, and not long after I passed my driver's licence test that, for the first time, I drove from Glenmorgan to Toowoomba by myself, with baby Colleen.

Maree told me not to drive into Toowoomba, "Think of Colleen, you cannot drive." Well, those famous last words! I packed some clothes for all of us and headed to Toowoomba, a three-hour drive away. I took my time and drove carefully, and I got there just fine. Colleen had slept all the way, so she was full of energy when we arrived.

But I was told off — again — by Maree, and accused of putting Colleen in danger by driving to Toowoomba. Remember, I was about 23 years old at this point, not an idiot, and yet again I was being yelled at, accused of putting my daughter in danger. I laugh about it now, but back then it was not a laughing matter.

When we got to the hospital to see Tony, oh how I wish the floor could have just opened up and let me fall through it! He was not in a good way, and his condition had deteriorated to the point that both sides of the family were called to come and see him.

Great! We had one child already, I was pregnant with our second child, and things were looking bad for Tony. Maree was there all the time talking to the doctors and telling the nurses what to do. I remember having an argument with a young, stuck-up doctor; I was fed up, so I said my piece too. He did not like being told a few home truths, so he tried to get me thrown out of the hospital. Someone had to do something! All the doctors were saying a lot, but were doing nothing, and Tony was getting worse. So, I lost it. And then to my surprise, Maree came into it and started speaking in medical terms. Well, that was it for me, I was lost, I couldn't understand what was being said — nothing.

Family members did come and see Tony but, fortunately, after I told the doctor off things changed and Tony's condition started to improve. After that incident I noticed the baby had stopped moving. I was told by a doctor at Toowoomba Hospital to go to Nambour and stay with Maree until the baby started moving again and I'd had a health check. Yes, I did not want to worry anyone because I thought Tony's health was more important, and I was trying to be superwoman.

So, I left Tony's bedside at Toowoomba Hospital and went to stay in Nambour. Tony had improved enough to get out of Toowoomba Hospital and go to Nambour on the 4th of November. He was not there 24 hours and on the 5th of November he was admitted to Nambour Hospital!

He was undernourished and had a huge blood clot where his kidney had been. After a considerable amount of time Tony recovered enough for us to return home to Glenmorgan.

In 1986 things were going okay; the time for the baby to be born was getting closer, and as we lived about a one-hour drive from Tara Hospital, I was admitted early for safety reasons. We had a few false runs, and then Rachel Lee was born on the 24th of February. At that time, it was the hottest day on record in Tara, and there was no electricity that day—so no air-conditioning either! I gave birth to Rachel and straight away, the electricity came on!

Home with Rachel, and life returned to normal—if you could call it that. Maree came to 'help', and yet again, in my own home I was told, "You need to do this," etc., etc. I was so fed up with all the control and being told I was no good! Shut up, Maree, or it is a fight!

Tony was working in the back paddock one day, when a battery blew up in his face and badly damaged one of his eyes. After going to the hospital and being admitted, and then needing time off work to recover, he resigned from the job at Glenmorgan.

***

It is funny now—but it wasn't then—while we were still living at Glenmorgan, people accused me of having a relationship with a bloke who worked on the next farm. I love rodeos, and this bloke said he competed in them. Oh boy, I was sucked in! It took a while to wake up to the lies. People can be so hurtful and cause so much trouble by surmising about what is going on.

Every weekend Tony and I would go to the pub for a drink or a meal and to socialise, and if there were any kids there, our kids would play with them. But on this afternoon I had had enough of the gossip and the accusations which were putting pressure on my marriage. Sitting in the public bar was this bloke, so I told Tony that I would be back in a minute.

So, into the bar I went, tapped this bloke on the shoulder and said, "Hi!" With that, I took his hat off his head, and oh boy, the bar went quiet. Well, let's say I said a few things, and told this bloke what I thought of him and his mouth. With that, I reached for his beer and emptied it over his head and in his hat. Then I put his hat on the floor and stood on it. A few mouths fell open, and I told him if he opened his mouth again and ran me down ... well, I won't repeat what I said. I heard not a word after that, but the whole district, and even the next town, heard of what went on in the pub.

Some people cannot accept that everyone is different; I could talk to men better than to women. But regardless, I was, and still am, being crucified because all I did was talk to that bloke.

We left the farm at Glenmorgan and we moved in with Maree at Nambour. She told me how to do nearly bloody everything! When it came to the kids, I *never* did a thing right—according to Maree. I could not wait to leave there, so when Tony said we had to go to Guyra in New South Wales for a job interview, I was happy.

He got the job, and we moved down there. Yet again, Maree came down to stay with us and it was, "Do that, do this!" It was my home, but it did not matter to her, and oh, the way she spoke to the shearers! The floorboards would not open up for me to go through them! I was so embarrassed, I walked away.

On the 5th of May 1989, our son Cody John, 'CJ', was born. That was the Labour Day long weekend in June, and a quarter of an inch of snow had fallen. Being a Queenslander, I had never seen snow before.

Colleen got Tony with the snow. Tony's brother and his wife and family came down to stay for the long weekend. The men had been drinking rum the night before, and Tony was a little *under the weather*, shall we say. Colleen called him to come outside, he came out and next thing, the cigarette that was in his mouth was on the ground, thanks to a direct hit from a snowball from Colleen—great aim! The snow did not stay around for too long so everyone, but me, had fun; I had a one-month-old baby wanting a feed.

Things happened and we moved back to Nambour to live with Maree.

In 1990, we moved into a house on Mapleton Road, Nambour, opposite Nana. Of course, Maree would come over to our house!

The girls caught the bus to school and we had to cross the road to the bus stop at the shop. Well, this day Rachel ran ahead, and a car came from nowhere. Fortunately, she was not hit, but the driver of the car was shaken up, and after I checked Rachel was unhurt, I spoke to the driver and apologised. Rachel never crossed a road again without holding on to my hand.

When Maree found out, Holy Mother, I got it again! "You should have been watching her!" On and on she went. Talk about making a person feel that they are not a fit parent; I questioned the incident repeatedly in my mind. No matter what we were doing it was never good enough for Maree. Like the time Tony and I bought a pool for Christmas for the kids and us. We spent many a night digging out the backyard for the pool, and Tony had already thought of what type of safety fence to put up. Oh no, nothing was good enough, "The pool is dangerous!"

Well, we finished building the pool and the safety fence. We spent a lot of time in the pool, and had great fun — and it was completely safe!

Now the house on Mapleton Road was an old one, built high off the ground at the back and the side. One day the windows were open and Maree and I were downstairs when I looked up and saw CJ standing on the dining room windowsill. Oh my God!! Well, Maree spoke to him while I raced up the back stairs and quietly walked through the house. It seemed like it took a long time until I grabbed CJ. He had pushed a chair up to the box freezer, climbed on top of it, and stood looking out of the window at everyone. Kids will be kids, but sometimes they do things that make your heart stop, and this was one of them. BUT I got the blame from Maree: "What was a chair doing near the freezer? He would be dead if he had fallen!" On and on, no matter that I already felt awful enough about it. My body was shaking, and the tears weren't stopping.

But my baby boy, my favourite—yes I admit that CJ was my favourite—could have died! That afternoon the freezer was moved, what a job, and I checked the whole house for anything near a window that a child could climb onto.

TWELVE | EARLY 1991

In mid-January 1991, something happened that I never thought possible. Tony hurt me. I won't say more, but the trauma and suffering caused me many lasting emotional, mental, and physical health problems.

I couldn't talk to Maree about it, so where could I go for help? The morning after everything happened, I rang my old friend, Mr L, in tears. He came to the house to find me curled up in a ball in the corner of the lounge room. He guessed what had happened, even though I would not tell him. I felt ashamed, and I was frightened. All I wanted was my Dad, but of course, he could not be there.

Mr L would pop in and check on me every morning to see if I was okay. He didn't want me to stay in the house, but I had nowhere to go, and no one to turn to. Tony accused me of having an affair with Mr L, but that was so far from the truth. And of course, Maree believed the worst. If she had only known what really had happened.

After about two weeks, I did seek professional help, and it was on that same day that Maree found out about what had happened. The counsellor had Maree on speaker phone at this appointment, and he was adamant that, for our own safety, the kids and I should leave Tony, *and Maree agreed to help.*

The counsellor did not think I was in a fit state to drive, and, yes, I probably should not have driven, but I had to get home before Tony did, to pack. It was not going to be easy to get everything packed for the kids and me in time. The only place I had to go was Maree's, which was my family home, the home that I grew up in. I had no money, nothing at all.

But did she really care? No, she just said *I* must have done something for Tony to do that to me. The counsellor I saw could not believe that there was no care or concern given to me by Maree.

Okay, so I got home and I had packed some of the kids' things, but not all of it, and I was packing some for me when Maree arrived.

"Leave the kids' stuff!" Why? You agreed to us all going to your place. I pleaded, saying, "I can't leave my kids, they are my world!"

"I can't take time off work to look after them, and you are not fit to look after them. You can get the kids later."

Much pleading and tears got me nowhere, so I went to live at Maree's and the kids stayed with Tony. As a mother, regardless of what is going on in your life, your children are the most important thing. Her words haunt me to this day. I wish I had stood my ground, but I was not well, and you did not argue with Maree. I felt there was no motherly concern from her in that moment, no hug, no reassurance, just orders to hurry up.

I lost my kids that afternoon, because their own grandmother, Maree, did not want to help them or their mother. Even to her dying day, Maree denied that she would not let me take the kids. She told all my kids that I left them, she never told them she refused to let them come with me. Even to the day she died, she never told them the truth.

It was so hard to keep on doing what she wanted. I was now 29 years old, and mentally I was a wreck. To be on my own, and to feel that I had no support, no caring, it was a lonely, dark place. My life with Tony had finished, but he had the kids. I fought to get custody of my kids for many years.

I never got custody of my kids because Maree refused to take them, even though she had previously agreed to it. She told my kids that I left them, which is so wrong—*she* refused them, not me. Regardless of what anyone says, I blame her for turning her back on her grandchildren. I cannot forgive, or forget, the stress and trauma Maree caused me by her own selfish ways.

It took many months, years even, for me to recover from what Tony had done to me. I had many sessions with a counsellor: many tears, facing my fears, questioning myself, and discovering that I did not have the skills needed to handle certain things. Because of the turbulent life I had led, I had problem after problem, and no guidance on how to deal with them.

Maree and I had a few counselling sessions together, and no matter what was said, she was in the right and I was in the wrong. Always. Always trouble, etc. When asked about leaving the kids, Maree became defensive and, again, it was about her and her work, and I was in the wrong. Christ, I couldn't do a bloody thing right in her eyes! After a while, Maree stormed out of the session, and we never had another one together after that.

But when I got home she accused me, "How dare you make a fool out of me! You are always causing problems, and I won't be made a fool of!"

Regardless, she kept on with the mental abuse for days and days.

THIRTEEN | LATE 1991

Somehow, I met 'Pauly'. He was a quiet person, lonely, funny, with a huge heart. He introduced me to tennis and indoor cricket. Tennis was a stress release. He always laughed at how I would run after the ball and hit it, and meanwhile land in the fence. As time went on, he got me playing indoor cricket, oh boy, there is nothing better than hitting the inside out of a ball when you are angry, hurt, depressed. It was great. I got on with many of the people down at cricket. I was not the best player, but I enjoyed it. It was time out from Maree and the constant degrading.

But I paid the price for putting my body on the line. One night I was playing mixed cricket. I put my left hand out to catch the ball, but my aim was off. The ball hit mid-way between my wrist and elbow. Well, everyone at cricket heard what I thought I had done. Thankfully, I had not broken it, but Christ, it was sore! No care from Maree concerning my injury. But that injury was the first of a few.

I have paid the price for dropping to my knees to stop many a ball. I have had one operation on the right knee but, unfortunately, because of certain things, I have never been back to get the left one done. Maree did not like that I was starting to go out instead of hiding in the house. Everyone thought I was in a relationship with this bloke. Hello people, I was *not* in a relationship; as the old saying goes, 'You can take a horse to water, but you can't make it drink'. Still, Maree was saying I should not be out with a man, I should not talk to them or see them, all they do is take you for a ride, and hurt you, and they are only after one thing.

Well, it is a decision you make, and you are the one who must live with it and take responsibility for your actions. Funny, how people jump to conclusions and, in my case, those conclusions were said to Maree, and she believed them to be true.

All Maree wanted was for me to stay home, not talk to men or have anything to do with them. It felt like I was a prisoner at times—and no way must I get out!

When I started working at the bowls club, that Pop had built on the weekends, I would work behind the bar and I really enjoyed it, talking with people, the laughs, and most of all learning new skills. Working at the bowls club gave me time away from Maree.

Maree was so mean, and she ran down every person I spoke to or had an association with. I met a guy, and he loved the beer. But of course, Maree let her view be known very strongly. I found I lost friends and acquaintances because of her and her strong, loud views. But I did not listen to that. I was around thirty years old, but still young. I decided I had a life to live. So yes, I met a couple of deadbeats.

At about the end of 1991 I went for a trip to Rockhampton, much to Maree's disapproval. I went up for a holiday and to meet a guy I had been talking to. Rockhampton was different to anywhere I had ever been. Life was great away from people who knew me.

I decided that I was going to move to Rockhampton. Oh my goodness, Maree went off like no one's business. She basically wanted me to become a nun and, because I had not, she was not happy, and some of the words she said still echo in my mind.

Words a mother should never say to her daughter.

Rockhampton was great, I moved around a bit there and finally moved to Yeppoon. I moved in with a lady called Lesley. Now, Lesley was great. I sat and told her everything that had gone on in my life and she was mad, upset, concerned. She did meet Maree, and that turned out to be a very heated meeting.

As time went on, she taught me cooking, etc., plus she introduced me to nightclubs. Her son would take me fishing. Life at that time was great, but I missed my kids. So, I contacted Tony about me having the kids in the school holidays at Yeppoon. 'Pigs would fly' before he would let me have the kids in Yeppoon!

Needless to say, I drank a lot of rum trying to ease the pain, but as I learnt later on in life, it does not work.

I missed my kids something bad. I went home a few times in the hope of seeing them, but as soon as Tony found out I was home he would take the kids away for the weekend. Did Maree ever go into bat for me and say something to Tony? Never!

So, time went on and life in Yeppoon was going great. One day in 1992, somewhere around August or September, I got a letter, Tony had filed for divorce and custody of the kids. To say I was not happy was an understatement. After everything, I had to go home to sort this out. So, in late September or early October, I said goodbye to everyone and my life in Yeppoon to go back to Nambour to fight divorce and custody battles.

I had to live at Maree's again. I got the night train from Rockhampton back to Nambour, and got in at 4 a.m. Maree was to look after the kids that night. About 7 a.m. or 8 a.m., she got a phone call from Tony, he said she did not need to look after the kids now because he was taking them with him for the weekend. He knew that I was back home in Nambour and he was adamant that I would not see the kids. Did she go into bat for me? No!

This started a lengthy and costly battle for custody and access, and divorce proceedings. When the legal costs reached approximately $50,000 I stopped fighting. I was paying for a solicitor out of what was the sickness allowance from Centrelink. It took me years, but I paid

Left Standing At The Fence

back every cent to the solicitor and to Maree, who had lent money to me.

On New Year's Eve 1993 I met up with a bloke I had been to school with. He moved into Maree's. Okay, it may not have been the right thing to do. We did a lot of fishing, but I had at last got to see the kids.

No matter what I did, nothing was good enough! Even after Tony's new girlfriend tried to run me over, did Maree do anything to help? Ha! Not on your nelly — blamed me again!

In January 1993, the divorce was finalised. Later that year Colleen came to live with me, and this did not make Tony happy. But I was happy. With what money I had, I paid rent, food, fuel, etc., plus put Colleen into marching. I gave her what I could, but that was not enough. And, of course, Maree had to interfere; I could not do a thing right.

FOURTEEN | 1993 to 1997

Aunty Carol and Bill and their girls lived not far from both Nana and us. Aunty Carol got a shock in 1992: she had cancer. We all thought she had beaten it, but then in about January 1993, it came back.

There is one day that I will never forget. One Friday I had to look after Aunty Carol. She was sick. Nana was down at the house, cooking and cleaning and looking after the girls, oh and the visitors.

But the worst thing was — and I did not for one minute say I did not want to — I had to look after Carol, she was my aunt. This meant feeding, clothing, bathing, and toileting. Now, I do not have any nursing experience, and we got through it, but the trauma of that day has never left me.

Aunty Carol would get cranky because I had to help her, and I felt like I was invading her privacy when I had to help her on and off the toilet. Many a time I went outside for a cigarette and cried. I was mad that Maree went to work and did not stay home and look after her sister. Maree was the nurse, not me. It was so awful to watch my aunt deteriorate before my eyes.

Maree came to Aunty Carol's at about 4 p.m. The doctor had been up during the day and said she needed to go to hospital, but Aunty Carol, being the stubborn person she was, would not go. But when Maree saw how much Carol had deteriorated, she got her to go to hospital. I said my goodbyes to Aunty Carol that day. I knew that I would not see her again.

Aunty Carol died on the 22nd of February 1993.

To add insult to injury, my now ex-husband and his new wife—who had been my closest friend—turned up at the funeral. I was mad as hell, I am sure there was fire coming from my eyes, I wanted them out, they were not family and did not belong there. I remember a mate taking me outside, I cried and cried.

It is unfortunate that we also lost Carol's youngest daughter to cancer, in 2011.

After a time, Colleen and I and this bloke moved out of Maree's to a house. Colleen and I did not stay with him for too long. No one touches, or talks to, my kids the way he did. I may not have had custody, but no one on this earth touches or speaks to my kids rudely; discipline is my right, not anyone else's. He crossed the line, so we moved out while he was at work. I thanked Maree for taking the morning off work to help. Colleen and I were back living at Maree's again.

The one thing that I am happy about is I made a friend for life. His sister, Ruby. We are nearly the same. Unfortunately, she and her hubby live six hour's drive away from me, so we keep in touch by talking on the phone, etc., but I wished that she lived a lot closer.

Again, I tried my best with what I had. But it was never enough, and all the time Maree would be on about how I should not be meeting men. Blah, Blah, Blah! I did not want to turn out like her.

Colleen and I had done okay. Things went up and things went down. However, I enjoyed the time with her; I tried to teach her what I had never been taught, but she is her mother's daughter. She can certainly have a temper, and when she uses that temper, my goodness, watch out!

There is a saying, *'Kids are not born with manuals, and you do the best you can'*. Usually, mothers are there to help you, to guide you. Not in my case.

What's the old saying? *'The apple doesn't fall far from the tree'*. Oh, how true this is.

As time passed, we moved out of Maree's house into a flat. What a great move. Colleen and I got on great; we had great neighbours, not far from school for Colleen.

The bloke I had been with had introduced both Colleen and me to darts, and we continued to play. I got the position of treasurer of the club, so my interest had grown and so did the lack of sleep.

My neighbours at our new place were top people: Carlie — what a great woman, funny, quiet, and great shoulders for tears. We are still friends today.

Andrew F — oh my goodness, this guy was unreal. Younger than me, but protective of both Colleen and me, even though he had a girlfriend. Some of the memories of our life in the flat can never be taken away from us. Andrew F got on well with all my kids.

In the end, Carlie and I would go out to the nightclub or to each other's place. Something happened and we moved into a house together. Party time—not really, because we were both quiet.

Carlie had a fall at work and ended up on her back on the lounge room floor for about three months. I looked after her and felt for her. She would crawl to the toilet because her back was so sore, and while she was not well, her boyfriend and her broke up. The house had changed for the worse. Carlie was so down because of breaking up with her boyfriend, and her back injury, that I met up with her boyfriend and had a talk to him.

That night he turned up with red roses in hand and they got back together! I was happy, even though I did not have a man in my life. Oh, I went out with different men, but nothing serious. I had not met the right man—yet.

During this time, I would get CJ and Rachel on access visits. It was hard because I did not know what to do. I did not want to say anything, or do anything, that would start Tony off again because the situation with him was not good. I loved seeing CJ and Rachel, and they loved the house.

In amongst everything, Maree would just turn up. Always, "What are you doing, when are you doing this?" On and on.

We got notice the house had been sold so we had to find another one. We got one further away from Maree. I gave Colleen some freedom, tried to live a life myself, but all the time Colleen was my first concern.

Carlie's boyfriend lived with us as well. Carlie and her boyfriend did their own thing, and after a while we all decided to go our own way. They got a little house in Nambour, and Colleen and I got a unit not far from them.

Because I loved dancing, I would regularly go to the Nambour RSL and listen to music or dance.

FIFTEEN | 1998 to 2002

Carlie and her boyfriend were married in 1998, and I had the joy and honour of being Matron-of-Honour. I helped Carlie with the craftwork she did for the wedding, such as the headpieces and baskets for the flower girls.

As Colleen got older she would dress the way no 16-year-old should. But she would not listen to me. So, after many arguments, I decided to move from Nambour, and I found a house in the small town of Mooloolah, west of Caloundra.

I shared this home with a chap, even though the story was I was in a relationship with him. That is far from the truth. One day he borrowed my car. He did something to it, and when I got home — thanks to a lift from someone — I found out he had done a runner. He had taken everything of his ... and some things of mine! The real estate agency was fantastic.

I had to ring Maree for help, but I was told off for moving to this town and leaving Colleen. I did not leave her in Nambour, like Maree put around! To this day people still believe her, and I am wrongly accused because of it.

I rented a home for Colleen and myself, she had a room in the house, I was giving her the freedom to travel on the train back to Nambour of a weekend, and to do as she wished. But to this day, she says I left her. I did **not** leave her, she chose to stay in Nambour, but she told everyone otherwise, including the neighbourhood and anyone who would listen.

It was at this time I had a bad car accident. Out of the accident, I was the only one of five to be taken to hospital. Thanks to the guard railing, the car did not run off the side of the road. The drop was approximately 50 feet down! I went into shock in my car, but what hurt was my back and neck. Every bump in the road between the roundabout and Nambour Hospital I felt because of pain.

There would be no more working for me from that time on. The accident changed my life. Rest! It is frustrating not being able to do anything. I can't even bend over and pick any thing up — and things like that.

If all this was not bad enough, I was still getting in trouble with Maree, **and** now everyone was looking down on me thanks to Colleen's mouth.

Because of the accident, I now have degeneration of the spine and problems with my neck. I also received whiplash in the accident, which has never been treated.

***

Back to Maree's to live. We cleaned the house in Mooloolah before moving out; Maree helped, but all the time she was complaining, running me down, saying I am trouble, and that I don't deserve my children. I was not looking forward to moving back, but I had nowhere else to go.

I was recovering from my accident when I got asked to come and play darts at the Nambour RSL. Anything to get me out of Maree's house! I found out I loved it. The group of people I played with were great, and we had a lot of fun.

This is where I met my second husband, Doug. Oh, what a mistake! But at that time I thought it was right. We would see each other at darts, and as time went on I would go to Cooroy to see him. After a time, just a short time, we were engaged.

Colleen, yet again, caused more trouble. At that time I was now living at Cooroy; Colleen had come up to live with us, but she did not like going to Noosa District High School. She wanted to go to Nambour High School. Back then, I couldn't find a way of making that work.

One day, Colleen did not come home from a weekend in Nambour. I rang her and asked her to come home. Not on your nelly! She was staying in Nambour with her 'friends'. No amount of talking was going to change this situation.

Doug and I had to take a washing machine to Maree in Nambour. We were just walking out the door when Colleen rang. I told her we were coming to Nambour and asked could I meet her somewhere. No, she wanted her stuff. I made a time later in the afternoon with her to come and get her things.

We got to Maree's, and Colleen rang my mobile number. She had broken into Doug's and wanted certain items. I cannot remember what they were, but I was pissed off she had broken into our house. Doug was not happy, and now Maree was blaming me for all of this.

I rang the police from my mobile phone to report the break-in. They advised that we must ring them after we got home to let them know what had been taken. We did not know how she got in, all the doors and windows were locked and intact. Later, we found out that she took out a window and got in that way. She had also let some other persons enter Doug's house, and she had been through *my* stuff.

Now that the police were involved, Doug and I decided she had to learn you cannot do that, so I put a charge of Break and Enter on her.

As it turned out — and for the life of me I do not know why the police believed her — she put a charge on me!

In the end, I delivered the items that I believed she wanted to the Nambour Police Station, and I got back some of the items she had taken from the house. I cannot, to this day, believe she was not charged with Break and Enter, but she did have her fingerprints taken and the 'riot act' read to her.

After that, Colleen would not talk to me. She hardly spoke to Maree, but would ask her for help. Maree always went on about how Colleen was making her look like a fool. How, I don't know. I think it was all in Maree's mind — was she becoming paranoid?

Doug and I were married in February 2001. Maree still had a part to play in our wedding and, of course, she did not like some of my choices or the way the reception was run. So sad, so bad! *At last I put my foot down!*

As time went on Rachel came to live with me, but she had a lot of trouble at school because of Doug's duaghters. Oh boy, did we have trouble. Even when Rachel joined the school band, she had to put up with Doug's girls again. She did well in the band but, like me, had a lot of trouble at school.

Then I had to go to hospital to have an operation. Knowing that Doug had children, I thought he would be capable of looking after Rachel while I was in hospital, and if anything went wrong, he would help her. Like hell, he was as useful as a wet paper bag! He did *not* look after Rachel. The poor child had health problems and he did nothing for her. He made her walk to school in an area where there were a lot of semi-trailers and cars on the road.

The worst was yet to come. An incident happened, which for legal reasons I cannot go into, but when I got out of hospital and I found out what had happened, I lost it, big time. The poor child was in hell.

I helped Rachel as much as I could. I took Rachel to the doctors and then down to the hospital, but there was a more serious problem which had to be dealt with, which Rachel had not told me about yet. I did what I could to help Rachel, but she had changed.

Then I found out what had happened. The phone call to Doug was not polite, to say the least. I was so angry I was physically shaking. In the end, I found out *exactly* what had happened, and that night he was told it was over. NO ONE goes near, disciplines, smacks, or does anything else to my children. He had broken a cardinal sin.

Therefore, within two weeks Rachel and I moved out and into a house not far from the high school. Doug and I could not speak to one another without my temper coming out. I blamed myself for what had happened, but I blamed him for not being a caring human. I was angry, upset, mad, and pissed off.

At that time, I had Rachel and CJ, and their behaviour was changing for the worse. So, I asked Andrew F, the guy I lived next door to in the flats, to talk to CJ.

We had to move out of that house into another one; it was a larger home, it was off the main road, and it had a good backyard.

Left Standing At The Fence

Over time, things went up and down. Then Colleen—who was now living in Ballarat, Victoria—came home. Oh me, as if I did not have enough problems! Colleen and I ended up having a massive argument. We were at somebody's home and, being that we were in someone else's house, I did not want to fight. She knew which buttons to push to get me mad, and she pushed the wrong ones. Words were exchanged; of course, I did not know what I was talking about, according to her. I took her phone off the table, I do not recall why, but the next moment I was bent over a windowsill, and my body had pushed out the flyscreen. Oh, the pain in my back!

I did my best as a mother, but this was not the first time Colleen had hurt me; and then to assault me verbally and physically, her own mother—that was the end as far as I was concerned. Everything she was doing to me was bringing back all the hurt I got from Maree. NO respect, no love, no care! I took Rachel and CJ and went home, thinking the air would settle and we could talk. Not on your bloody nelly. Colleen came home and started up again, but this time I told her if she laid a hand on me, I would be calling the police. Enough is enough! And where is the respect?

A week later Colleen left and went back to live in Ballarat. Home was okay for a while, BUT when I went to Kilkivan to pick CJ up from Tony, it turned into another disappointment. I have since found out that Colleen rang Tony and told him a load of lies. So, Tony kept CJ! The old Commodore car I had then heard many a swear word said all the way from Kilkivan back to Gympie!

I had gone through the court system, and had done whatever Tony asked, but it was not good enough, he was still dictating to me regarding my children.

With CJ gone, we moved into a unit. Rachel had started a job — I think it might have been a school-based traineeship — at IGA in Cooroy.

She had given up the band, and was excelling at her job in retail. She made me proud. I told her many times how proud I was, and am, of her — but these days she won't talk to me.

Do not count your chickens too early. I was there for Rachel, but now I was starting to live my life. I have never put any of my kids behind anything or anyone; my kids have always been number one to me. But, having said that, all my kids believe I put them last.

I would go dancing with a friend on a Friday and/or Saturday night just to get out. However, going to RSLs by yourself can get very lonely.

I had been having a lot of trouble with the car. Nana and I had spoken about it, she was worried that something might happen and I would need to get Rachel to a hospital. I agreed I would come down and talk to her about it. She even offered to lend me the money to get a car, she said, "Come down and we will sort everything out."

Left Standing At The Fence

I was going to see Nana on the 28th of August 2002. It was a Thursday, and at about 7 a.m. the phone rang; it was Maree, and she told me Nana had died. That alone was a massive shock; yet another person I loved and looked up to, had left me.

I told Maree I would come down to Nambour. Like hell, stay at home. Why? Wendy helped Maree with everything!

I lost my Nana and got pushed out. All my life it has been me on the outer. It really hit home this time, and the funeral, oh my goodness. I did not want to sit at the front of the funeral home but I was ordered to. Because of my love for Nana, of course the tears came freely.

"Stop your crying, you are making a fool out of me," came out of Maree's mouth. I could not believe my ears. I cannot remember who went up to the coffin with me, but they had to help me back to my seat.

When we went outside, I walked away from everyone, Nana was gone, another hole in my life. And I was still upset at Maree. At the graveside, I walked to Dad's grave, sat down, and cried. I did go to Nana's but not while everyone was there. The one thing I wish Nana had taught me was to make her Christmas pudding in the rag, and her Christmas cake.

From the time of Nana's death, the way the family — or so-called family — treated me, hurt me deeply. The cruel words, feeling unwanted, being degraded, rundown, and excluded, and not being allowed at the family home. Moreover, it goes on and on.

I did not realise it at that time, but I wish I had seen it coming, or that someone would have said something to me. It may have stopped many mental problems, which have arisen from feeling excluded from the family.

I grieved in my own way. Back in the unit at Cooroy, I lost a lot of weight, smoked more, and drank my coffee. I lost so much weight my doctor was ready to put me in hospital. Not on your nelly, I was not going to hospital. No fucking way I was going to the same hospital where Maree worked!

I had trouble sleeping because my relationship with Rachel had turned, and was going downhill so fast I could not do anything to stop it. I rang all the helplines looking for some type of support. In the end I was told if she was not obeying the house rules, and did not wish to, I should tell her she needed to find somewhere else to live, and give her a timeframe. Oh, that sounded harsh, but it had got to that.

I did not know it at the time, but Rachel was ringing Maree and talking to her about everything. Yet again, I was the person who knew nothing, and did not know how to treat a person!

Matron-of-Honour at Carlie's wedding, 21st November 1989

SIXTEEN | 2002

One day in 2002, sitting out in the sun, doing a lot of thinking, I came to a decision—I deserved to start a new life. I was not going to sit in a unit and become an old woman who was as sour as a lemon. I met a few men, but nothing came of it.

Read many an advertisement, rang a few, but no one stirred that special feeling until ...

I was reading a story in—I think it was—'Just Life' magazine, where a woman could not meet anyone, so she sat down and wrote a 'pros and cons' list.

I started thinking, 'Why the hell not? I have nothing to lose.' I was amazed when I finished it. Could I ever meet anyone who would fit this list? So, out of desperation, I joined a dating club. I gave the lady there a brief description of the man I would like to meet, and because I was 40 years old then, I gave a similar age range, *but no more than five years younger than me.*

The first man I met did not even come close, then I got a phone call from the lady at the dating club. She rang me because they had a new man on their books meeting my description, BUT he was nine years younger than me.

After a lot of chewing my tongue and thinking, I said, "Okay, I will meet this man."

It was the best thing I ever did!

That man became my husband. Brian and I were married on the 11th of November 2003. We have split up a few times and then got back together again, and in 2018 we decided to split up as a couple for good, but we have stayed friends ever since.

We spoke on the mobile phone for about a month or two and Telstra loved us for that. My mobile bill for one month was approximately six hundred dollars ... oh well, we were getting to know one another.

Finally, we met. I did not get home until 2.30 the next morning. That was Saturday; Monday night we met again and this time it was 4.00 am. Oh, time to me was nothing. Brian ended up coming up to my place, but he slept on the couch because he could see I just needed company because of all that was going on with Rachel.

He worked driving a Bobcat for a business in Brisbane. Even though we had only been together a few weeks, Brian could see what Rachel was putting me through. Oh, Rachel was not happy, the spotlight was off her. She could slam doors, and she had a mouth.

Then one day did it for me; I was so mad I tried to throw my cigarettes and lighter through the bedroom door. Well, they did not ever get there, they ended up under a cupboard and that added insult to injury. This made my temper start to rise even more. I tried to reason with Rachel, but to no avail. She tried to slam her bedroom door as I went out of her room, and it hit my back. That did it! I asked for an apology, as she knew about my back injuries, but no way would she apologise. So after a few words, she was told, "You have three weeks to get out!"

Brian came and told me to go and make a coffee; he tried to talk to her, but to no avail as well.

"You have three weeks to get out," Brian told her.

"You can't tell me what to do, you are not my father!" Rachel screamed at him.

With that, I told Rachel that Brian had my permission, and I got a mouthful back from Rachel.

I was ropeable, so I went out on the back verandah of the unit. Next, I felt a hand on my right shoulder. My bad temper was going like a steam train; I spun around with my right fist in motion ready to smack this person. It was Brian and, thankfully, he has long arms, so my fist did not connect with him.

Rachel left saying something, and running me down, and the last thing she said was exactly like Maree had said many years ago, plus she called me a slut.

I do not know how, but she came back the next night and told me she had a place to go. Hey, that is only 24 hours. Next was the packing. "You take only your stuff, I will give you some linen and I will give you some kitchen stuff as well," I said to Rachel, trying to help her.

I got a mouthful back from Rachel, all the accusations under the sun. Maree rang me, and was mad with me and told me off. All I wanted to do was to scream. I cannot make anyone happy; I must bend and scrape to everyone and what they say.

Brian and I went down to his Mum's and Dad's place at Warana. He took me over to the beach and we walked and walked. I would look at the waves and wanted to just float out to sea, but then I felt Brian's strong loving arms around me.

When we entered the beach, we came in at entry 31, and we had walked all the way down to entry 38. Sitting on the sand, "Well, are you going to marry me?" Brian said, out of nowhere.

"Ah boy, can I think about it for a moment?" I said in surprise. Because I had been married and divorced twice, I was cautious.

Then I replied, "Yes, I will marry you". This was the 15th of December, so yes, I had only been seeing Brian for about six weeks. Before you shake your head, remember this man already had helped me, accepted me for me, and was accommodating that I had children and a grandchild. (Colleen had given birth to Kelly on the 19th of September 2002.) And he was fine with all of it.

We did not tell Brian's parents until Christmas Day.

Christmas Day with Maree, oh why did I go?

"You should not be seeing a man, what about your kids? You kicked Rachel out. You should be working out what is wrong with you. All your kids have left you. You are not a mother!"

Enough! I am out of here.

I rang Brian and went down to his place. We did not know it, but his Mum, Hazel, had guessed that we had got engaged. She was happy for us, but she was losing her 'baby boy', who was now 31 years old. We spoke to Mum and Dad, and decided that I would move in with Brian at his Mum's and Dad's house. Rachel had moved out, so I could not afford the unit on my own, and travelling from Cooroy to Warana was too far.

We decided on a twelve-month engagement, and the twelve months went by quickly. When it came time to decide on whom to invite to the wedding, I hit a brick wall.

None of my children wanted to talk to me, Maree was mad with me, and I knew she did not agree with me marrying Brian, so I spoke at length with Hazel. I sent an invitation to Maree, but not to my children.

I got a phone call from Maree; she could not come because she was getting something done to her eye and could not drive. What a lie, she could have come; she had the eye operation done weeks before. Well, Brian got a phone call from Rachel because she was not speaking to *me* — she was not happy about not getting a wedding invitation.

For once this was going to be MY wedding and, of course, Brian's. In among wedding plans, and Brian working in Brisbane, we decided to move to Capalaba to be closer to his work.

We rented a caravan for a month or two before we bought our own. It was not much, and needed renovations badly, but it was home. **Our** home.

We moved into our home on the 25th of July 2002. The date is ironic: the 25th of July is the same date I married Tony. So, we moved all our belongings from Warana to Capalaba so I could set up our new home, as well as still organise our wedding! Somehow I got there; I did a lot of planning and most of the work, as Brian was working long hours.

I spoke to my brother, Keith, and asked him to give me away. Keith was so honoured. He was so happy I had asked him, and he hugged me so tightly.

On the wedding day, we could not have been more proud, Keith and I walking up the pathway to Brian.

"Dad would have been proud of us," I said.

"He would have," Keith replied, "and I am proud too, do not start crying or you will start me off." Out of concern, my little brother asked me, "Hey, you sure of this?"

"I have never been surer, thanks little brother for caring."

It felt funny at the wedding, it was Keith and me from my side of the family, and about forty from Brian's side, but Keith fitted in.

After the wedding, Keith and I took a time-out. We spoke about our Dad, and unfortunately, Keith did not remember him because he was only two or three months old when Dad died. But Ron Lawlor was still his dad, and Keith was my brother.

The time with Keith, having people there who cared about Brian and me—our wedding day was a great day! And Maree never even saw the wedding photos.

We honeymooned in Ballarat at Colleen's. We did the stupid thing and drove straight through, boy were we tired. We arrived at Colleen's place, and I got a hug from her as though nothing had gone on before. Next, I met my first granddaughter, Kelly. Oh, my heart was in my mouth, she was gorgeous. Kelly was a Poppa's girl while we were in Ballarat, and this didn't make Colleen happy. We had seven days there, and it hurt when it came time to leave, but we had to get back to Brisbane for Brian to start work. I loved meeting Kelly. She will always be special to me!

Keith giving me away at my wedding to Brian

Brian and me on our wedding day, 22nd November 2003

Brian, Keith, and me, happy together

I love this photo of Keith and me

SEVENTEEN | 2003 to 2005

After moving from Cooroy to Warana, I did not have communication with Rachel. It hurt like hell; I love my daughter. Regardless, I could not take the yelling, the screaming, the name-calling, and the disrespect she gave me all the time. During this time, Rachel started a tight relationship with her grandmother, Maree.

I am the first to say I am happy about that, IF it was a true bond. Oh, Rachel is smart. She was still working at IGA, and one day she collapsed out the front of the store. Maree helped her and took her to a specialist. When I asked Maree what the outcome of the specialist appointment was, she said Rachel had told her she was to tell me nothing. Oh my God, you are supposed to be a mother and care, why can't you tell me? I am Rachel's mother! I found out that Rachel was — I do not know — sort of blackmailing Maree. It got too much. Is Rachel okay? No. What can I do? Leave her alone.

This family was driving me to the point of exploding!

As the years passed, Rachel married and I was not invited to the wedding. Yes, it hurt, and even today, I do not know why I was not invited. To say I was considerably hurt, upset, and angry would have been an understatement! I was Rachel's mother and I deserved to be there. The injustice of her actions! Guess who helped Rachel, and was Mother-of-the-Bride? Yes — Maree! Rachel married a guy, they lived in Toowoomba, and I was never invited up to their place.

In 2004, Colleen rang me and told me she was having problems with the guy she was with in Ballarat, and she wanted to come home. We spoke about how she could get home; home being the caravan Brian and I lived in at Capalaba. She was going to come up on a 'holiday', but not go back. She started packing and making plans, but not exactly saying when she would be back.

Next thing, I got a phone call from Colleen. She was upset and angry, she could not leave Victoria with Kelly, and she had to go to court to get permission to leave the state with her.

Brian and I drove down to help her. We went to court with her, as any parent would do to help their daughter. The judge, and I do not remember his name, had the hide to say to me, "You only want to start up a mother-daughter relationship with Colleen, and that is the reason you want her home."

I was not very polite or calm when I spoke to the judge. I did not swear, but he knew I was not happy, to say the least. I reported that judge for the way he spoke to Colleen and me on that day.

We had to come home for Brian's work, so Colleen found out where she could move to while all the court action was being decided. At the end of 2004, we picked Colleen and Kelly up from Brisbane Airport.

The arrangement was for she and Kelly to live with us until she got the money to move out.

The best plans always seem to dissolve very quickly. As she had been talking to John, who lived two doors down from us, while she was in emergency care in Ballarat, Colleen moved into his van about a week after moving home to us. Our relationship was not the best, and it was very strained when we did talk. I have since found out that Kelly's dad never gave permission for his daughter to leave Victoria.

In March 2005, I got a phone call from Maree, "Have you heard from Keith lately?"

"No, why?"

"It is in today's paper, a man named Keith was killed," Maree said.

"You sure of the name?" And with that she read me the newspaper clipping.

My heart hit the ground. No, it can't be Keith! I have lost Dad, not him too.

"I will ring Keith's phone and see if I can find out what is going on, ring you back later." With that, I rang Keith's phone number.

The lady he was with answered the phone. "Do not tell me my brother is dead," were the words out of my mouth.

"I am so sorry, yes, Keith was killed last night." With that, she told me how he was killed and all about what the ambulance crew went through trying to save Keith's life.

We spoke on the phone for quite a while, and she explained everything she knew about the accident; she told me that she would ring me and let me know when the funeral was.

I can't remember whether I went down the three steps or over the verandah. The tears were streaming down my face and I was shaking. Colleen lived only two caravans down, so it did not take me long to get beside her van, and I just called for her. From the tone of my voice, she ran out. I had trouble telling her.

I finally got it out that Keith had been killed. All we could do was stand in the middle of the road and cry and hug one another. A lady who lived opposite Colleen came out of her van and we told her. Colleen asked me if I had rung Brian; this I had yet to do.

I went home and got my mobile phone and sat on the front steps of the van.

"Hi, honey."

"Babe, what's the matter? Stop crying, what's the matter, is Colleen there?"

Left Standing At The Fence

"Keith is dead, he got killed last night!" I somehow got it out.

"I am coming home, let me tell the blokes, and I will be home. Go down to Colleen's until I get there," Brian said.

"No, I will be here at home, I am okay. See you when you get home."

My little brother, the smile he had on his face all the time, the jokes, the white teeth ... gone. Why? Why? It is not fair!

At Keith's funeral, I met up with Tracey for the first time in thirty-three years. Not the best time to catch up with someone. But Tracey came and looked for me, and all she could say was she was sorry for everything. I never did, and still do not, hold Tracey accountable or blame her for anything. I told her this, and all we did was hug.

Brian and I went and said goodbye to Keith. He was so peaceful in his fishing clothes with his thongs plastered with sealant. I cried my eyes out. But I got to say goodbye to my little brother.

The funeral was a big one, and as I did not know much about Keith—owing to Maree keeping us away—I learnt a lot about my brother. The funny bugger, who got lost at sea, the guy who loved old farm machinery and country music.

Now I had to grieve over losing Keith, but I had a rock, I had Brian. Even though he did not know Keith that well, Brian felt the pain of his passing.

Part of a newspaper clipping about Keith's fatal accident

'FREAK accident ... a 30-year-old man died on Monday night following an accident which occurred while he and his friends were landfilling on a Sunshine Coast property. They had been using two mini tip trucks at the Lake Coorolba [sic] property when one of them became bogged. As they attempted to tow the truck free, a tow hook flew off, hitting the man in the stomach. He suffered internal injuries and was airlifted to the Royal Brisbane and Women's Hospital where he died late Monday night. Picture: Jason Dougherty'

Source newspaper unknown

I later learned that Keith was helping friends free a bogged truck just after 6 pm on a property at Lake Cooroibah when the bolts holding the metal towing hook under the front of the truck sheared off. The result was the hook was sent flying and, even though Keith was standing ten metres away, the hook went flying into Keith's lower abdomen causing fatal internal injuries.

We left the funeral and came back to Capalaba. We spent a few days keeping to ourselves, then Brian went back to work. That was March, and in May Brian went back to work for his old employer. Things were going okay, if you can call not having a proper relationship with your children that.

Beau was born in October 2005. I took Colleen to the hospital, all the time worried as she was having contractions, and the last thing I wanted was to have the baby born in the car! Beau arrived about at six that night.

During these years, Rachel, CJ, and Colleen were not talking to me. I was a help to Colleen, I wanted to be there to help her, but I was not wanted.

It got to the stage I could not look at any photo of the kids without ending up in tears, and asking the questions: What did I do wrong? Why won't they have anything to do with me?

Poor Brian, who had never had children, was right amongst all this. He was my sounding board, and it was not fair on him, me being upset, and him not knowing what to do.

EIGHTEEN | 2005 to 2006

In November 2005 Brian came home from work and said we had to pack and be in Port Douglas in three days' time for him to start work there. What? You never asked me about going away to work.

"You are going with me, the boss has given his permission," Brian said. Now I think we left on the 18th. Okay: take clothes, linen, cutlery, and so on. Go and buy handheld UHFs, and pack the car.

What a drive! With a fully loaded four-wheel drive, towing a Dingo with all the different buckets and blades. The chap that lived behind us was going up to work there as well. He was driving up in a fully-loaded work ute. We stopped at Mackay and Townsville. It was a long drive up, and we had already decided on the fuel stops.

Port Douglas was different: the heat, the town. But the worst was yet to come. On the third night, the chap who came up with us, had been smoking cannabis in his motel room. Before Brian got a chance, I did my block, so the air between the three of us was not relaxed and happy.

It did not help that the accommodation was totally wrong. We could not have spent two years in that place. Brian rang the boss to sort something out, and he said yes, if you can find a place in a certain price bracket you can move. We did, and we moved within two days.

The other chap did not learn from me doing my block. In the new place, which was beautiful, he was again smoking in his room. Now, his window backed onto the owner's back door. This had to stop now! Brian ended up taking him to Cairns and putting him on a bus. Good riddance, we thought.

But when the bloke got home all he did at work was trying to ruin Brian's reputation. Oh, I could not wait for Easter and for us to go home, I was going to stop this. Well, I missed out on that because the bloke had moved on. Damn! Brian and I kept going, with different workers, but the job got done.

In among all this I started to study a Certificate III in Business Services.

I got my driver's license in 1985, and had never had a ticket, of any description, until one day when we were on our way back to Brisbane for Easter. Coming down a hill outside Childers, I did not see the speed camera on the side of the road. I did not think anything of it until we got our mail from down in Brisbane a bit later.

Because of the length of time it took to get my mail, the ticket was now 'on demand'. I could not believe I got a speeding ticket! I rang up the transport office and explained the situation, and I was able to pay the ticket off. To date, I have not had another ticket.

In August 2006, Brian and I had to go to Hervey Bay for Brian to do a job there. Pack up and move again.

Brian rang me one morning, "Can you come over and take me to hospital? I have chest pain!"

"Okay, you alright? Why don't you ring an ambulance?"

"No, I will be okay, just come over," Brian said in a funny voice.

Now, the one time when I wanted the road to be clear, with no red lights or slow cars, it was that day. But no way, I got every damn red light, the traffic was like peak hour, and this was at 10 am! I finally got there and, fortunately, the trip to the hospital was quicker.

"Your husband looks like he may have had a heart attack." What? He is only 35 years old! Next minute the doctor came back with paperwork in his hand. "You have had a massive angina attack; it shows signs like a heart attack, but it is not one." Now, in between the doctors checking Brian out, I went out to the car for a smoke and to ring his boss.

When we found out what had happened, and what was going to happen, I rang the boss back. "He will be released tonight if everything is alright, but he will be off work for about a week."

Brian did not stay home for as long as the doctor told him. Back to work.

While we were there, Rachel and her husband came up. They were moving to Sydney and joining the Muslims. Now let me say this, everyone has a right to his or her own religion, but I disagreed with it so much. When she moved to Sydney, I did not see her, I got the occasional phone call and most of the time they were not nice conversations.

Now someone else was going to be finishing off the job at Hervey Bay, so before going back up north we had a few days with Brian's family, then headed back up to Port Douglas.

NINETEEN | 2007 to 2008

In January 2007, we were packing up to leave to come home to Brisbane. It had been pouring rain, and I had been listening to the radio to find out about the flooded roads. We woke up the next morning and Brian went over to work and came back.

He asked me, "Do you know another way around Townsville? The main road is flooding."

"No, but let's get the map out."

Finally, we decided to go from Cairns to Charters Towers, down to Rockhampton, then on home to Brisbane. We let our new puppy, 'Lord Jackson', out to go to the toilet, and then we set off. Lord Jackson was a purebred Maltese terrier, only six weeks old.

The road to Charters Towers, oh my, you did not dare put both wheels off the bitumen. Thanks to the UHF, I spoke to some truck drivers, and they let us know how the road was ahead. We had to go through floodwaters, but we got through okay. We were the last vehicle into Charters Towers that day, and the last one out the next morning.

We left Charters Towers at 9 a.m., and drove all day. We could not find a place to stay in Rockhampton, and even though we both were so tired, we kept going.

Outside Rockhampton we couldn't find Lord Jackson in the car. Oh hell! We pulled off the road, and started unpacking the car. Well, he was down under stuff behind the passenger seat!

Lord Jackson

Repack the car and away we go. At 3 a.m., the next morning, we pulled into Brian's Mum's and Dad's home at Warana. Totally exhausted, longing for a shower and a hot cup of coffee.

Back home, and it was back to work for Brian. For some reason, things between Brian and me were not as good as they should have been. In Port Douglas, Brian had told me he did not love me anymore. What a shock, I did not see that coming, I thought everything was fine! This was the main reason for us leaving Port Douglas.

In June 2007, I decided enough was enough. I was sick of the stories and the lies, so I looked into finding out all I could about my Dad. Now, Maree was not going to help because of her feelings towards Dad, even though he had been gone for many years. I looked to an aunt, who I had never really got on with, trying to find out information, and she was cautious.

Where do these people get off? He was *my* dad, alive or passed away, and there was a void in my life that I wanted to try to find the answers to.

On the internet, first thing that came up was his grave and the cemetery. I was determined to find out things, so out of desperation, I wrote to Maree. I got a letter back; let us say that, again, I was in the wrong for asking for information.

I got from her what the solicitor had not shredded, as there had been no activity on the account for over seven years. I did not get the original, or even a copy, of Dad's death certificate, but to my amazement there was information about 'carnal knowledge'.

What? I had never known about this! This got me digging further, and a friend who was a researcher told me about the State Archives. Oh, what a wonderful place.

On the internet, I found the State Archives page, did the search and, hello, yes there was a file. It was the file of Maree and Dad's divorce proceedings. Now, to get divorced back in 1974 was not like it is today. Back then it was under the *Matrimonial Causes Jurisdiction*. The file had everything. Additionally, on a microfilm I found out that the spelling of Dad's surname changed when he started school. Dad was enrolled in Brooloo State School in 1944, aged six years and two months. The surprising thing is, when he was enrolled—according to the microfilm at the State Archives—his name was entered as **Lawler**, Ronald Keith, not **Lawlor.**

All the papers were there, and it made very interesting reading. Now, at the State Archives building it is like a library. There is to be no noise. Well, I was reading through the papers and I let out, "holy mother!" I could not believe what was in those papers.

Unfortunately, there are a few things I have not been able to find out, and I will never be able to, as we are going back to the early 1970s. It has always been very hard for me. What is wrong, why don't people want to tell me about Dad? And worse still, it is as if *no one* wants to tell me about him. My temper was rising with no one wanting to tell me *anything*.

I continued with my search, and in about July, Brian and I separated. It was so hard to do normal daily things. Again, my life has gone downhill. Again I am losing someone I love. What is wrong with me?

Brian and I attended counselling and we got back together twelve months later. During that time, I did not hear from any of my children, and even though I was seeing Brian every day, life was very lonely. I did not know who to talk to, I could not talk to Maree, or Brian's Mum, Hazel. Some of Brian's family were not happy with me. Oh well, they did not know the truth.

In early 2008 we got some devastating news. The rock, the glue of Brian's family, his mother — Hazel — had leukemia, and the doctors had given her six to nine months to live. So, after that Brian's Mum and Dad went on trips, and lived every day to the full.

Late in July 2008 we got a phone call. "Mum is in hospital and all the family have been called in." This did not sound good. The doctors did not expect Hazel to live another twenty-four hours. Now, I still had the occasional phone call with Colleen, so I rang her up to tell her. Both Brian and I were a mess, so I asked her to drive us up to the Sunshine Coast to see Hazel for the last time.

I grabbed some clothes for both Brian and me, and we headed up to the coast. We got to Dad's and were told we had to urgently get to the hospital, NOW! We quickly organised the cars and set off; we went just around the corner, Brian's niece pulled up in her car with Brian's sister Jenny in it, and she said, "We have to get to the hospital in a hurry, things are not good." One thing I will never take away from Colleen is that she can *drive*. Drives fast and safe.

When we got to the hospital we went up to see Mum. Brian and I had only just got back together and even on her deathbed, when we told Mum, she was happy and she squeezed our hands. She was in a lot of pain. The rest of the family arrived to see her; only two people at one time were allowed into the room. Dad was a mess, as well as you would expect for a couple who have been together for fifty-odd years. I said goodbye to Mum, and left Brian with her for a private moment.

We had organised that we all would come up to the hospital at 9 a.m. the next day. Brian and I and Colleen were staying at Dad's. Brian rang his work and told them what was happening, and they were great, very understanding. Colleen rang her work as well.

About 8.30 the next morning we were all ready to go, and were just waiting for everyone else to come to the house first. Then we got a message not to come to the hospital yet. This was strange.

At about 9 a.m., Jenny and Linda, Brian's sisters came through the side gate. Tears were flowing down their faces, and they asked, "Where is father?"

I knew what had happened. Mum had passed away. Yet again, I have lost an important person in my life. Grieving, I had to put my emotions aside to help Brian and his Dad. Really, I did not grieve for Mum until about a month later.

We all went up to the hospital and spent time with Mum and said our goodbyes. Brian and I said our goodbyes with a lot of tears. Colleen went in by herself, she did not want me with her, and she grieved in her own way. She had to go home as she had to get back to work, but would be back up for the funeral.

Dad was specific about what plates and cups were to be used for the cuppa tea after the funeral. I did not mind one bit helping him, in a way I had shut down. It was easier for me, but on the inside, I was a complete and utter mess. It brought back all the memories of Dad, Keith, and Nana.

The funeral was very emotional, and during the funeral, I cuddled Brian, crying myself as well. It was extremely hard to see Mum being driven away in the hearse.

It took time, but Brian and I were closer than before, and we always told each other that we loved each other. He would go quiet, which was expected; he is the baby of nine, 'Mums boy'. I put my grief and emotions to the side for Brian and Dad. It has been a while now since we lost Mum, but she is still alive in our hearts.

Brian and I went over to visit CJ, my son, but nothing had changed with him. He now was living with his girlfriend; I didn't like her and she didn't like me. He was still working at the power station. He was polite, but he did not talk much. I got sick of asking the questions: How have you been? How is work? What have you been doing? I even asked him how his dad was.

After about an hour, I decided it was enough, Brian and I left. It had taken us three hours to get there, and I was disappointed that CJ did not want to talk, find out what was happening in our lives, or how I was. He had not changed, he was still lying to my face, making up stories. We had not yet driven out of the town he lives in, and he was on the phone to Maree. Now for many years Maree had been helping CJ with food, money, etc. She had replaced me; no wonder my son did not want anything to do with me.

I have always given, or done, what I could for CJ — but it was never enough!

TWENTY | 2008 to 2009

Some time in 2008, Colleen and John got engaged. Brian and I were happy for them, and Colleen and I had started talking again. I was very careful in what I said, as I did not want it to end in a fight, and miss another wedding! Brian and I went with her to a bridal dress shop.

"I only have a budget of $1500," Colleen said.

There was not a lot in that price range, and what was there she did not like. The gown she did like was way out of her price range. After about an hour, Brian said, "Get Colleen to try this one on."

The first thing she did was look at the price, and she said, "No." I knew Brian had something up his sleeve. "Just try it on," were his words to Colleen.

She did try it on, and when she walked out of the fitting room, we both held our breath. She looked beautiful! The downer, it was the only one left and it was too small for her.

"Are you able to let it out?"

Fantastic, it had huge seams in it, but it had beadwork on it too.

"Do you think you can lose the weight or do you want to let it go?" I asked Colleen.

"I can lose the weight," Colleen said to us.

Next problem was the cost of the dress.

"Don't worry about it, I will buy it for you," Brian said.

Colleen is not his daughter, and for him to pay for a wedding dress for her just blew me away.

"I will only accept this if you walk me down the aisle and give me away," Colleen said.

Thank the good Lord I was sitting down, otherwise I would have fallen down.

Next came the jewellery, stuff for her hair, and my dress. What do I wear? I had no idea; I had not even thought about myself yet. We had a look, and I found a nice dress. So far, we had Colleen's dress, my dress, accessories for her hair, her jewellery, and my hair accessory.

Then, we heard a little voice, "Nana, I like that dress, can I have it?" We all smiled, and I asked Colleen, "What are the kids going to be dressed in?"

We bought the dress for Kelly, and Colleen purchased her shoes. Recalling, Brian and I had a bill of $3500. I swallowed hard and looked at Brian with my eyes saying, 'How can we do that?'

Thankfully, the shop allowed us to lay-by everything.

All the men, including Brian, got their suits from the same shop. Colleen was lucky to find an outfit for Beau online, and he looked so cute in his little suit.

Owing to how Maree had controlled and run my wedding, I was not going to do that to Colleen. Even though, both Brian and I had an input as we were paying for most of it.

Colleen and John made most of the decisions about the wedding, but one week out Colleen came over to us in tears. "Can you help me, please, and pay for the reception? John's family have pulled out of paying for it and we don't have the money." I have since been told this was lies. Hmm, reminds me of someone.

I first scratched my head thinking, how the hell were we going to do this, as we ourselves were in so much debt. We both ended up increasing the limit on our credit cards.

"Okay, we have the money to pay for the reception, when do you have to pay for it?"

Overall, we paid for Colleen's wedding dress, Kelly's dress, the reception, and — since the best man did not organise it and people were already coming — we paid for part of the bucks' night. Additionally, we paid for Colleen and John to have a honeymoon, too.

Some people may say that is what parents do, alright, **but** to be spoken to rudely in front of people, to **demand** certain things when she was not paying for them, to *not* include me in a family photo, but get one of Brian and the grandkids, and to not be thankful for everything we had done — oh that *really* hurt!

BUT the worst thing was, she was too gutless to speak up when I was made a fool of by certain people!!

Colleen and John were married on the 15th of November 2008.

So, after she came back from the honeymoon, I would be polite just to see my grandchildren. Oh, there were the phone calls asking for help, like when John had an accident in her car and wrote it off.

We were still in our caravan, and there were new managers at the park. Everyone talked to everyone, and many people did not agree with certain things. In early 2009, the new manager of the park knocked on our front gate. Jackson was beside me.

"You have a problem with me?" the manager said in a very angry voice.

"No, I don't," I replied, and with what followed, I could not stop shaking and crying. He threatened Jackson, and me, and he degraded me.

I rang Brian at work, and to say he was not happy would be an understatement. When he got home, he went and faced the manager. Oh, the blame was put on me, of course.

"I don't care, the caravan is for sale, and we are getting out of this dump. Don't go near my wife again," Brian told the manager.

I rang a few real estate agents, and finally found one who sells caravans. The agent had a woman in mind already. Oh, to get out of the park! We sold the van and left the park in May, and we moved into a unit at Eagleby.

Life was okay, and being down at Eagleby we did not get the calls asking for help so much. I started having counselling for what the caravan park manager had done.

I was told, "You have Post Traumatic Stress Disorder. PTSD."

Oh, great, let's add this to the long list of health complaints I have already. More counselling, more tears, more reliving all my childhood.

I was still doing some research into Dad, so I had been in contact with the manager of the cemetery where he is buried. Maree was the burial rights holder to Dad's plot, but she was not looking after the headstone or the grave. Not many people are aware of the responsibilities and legalities regarding burial plots. If you pay for a burial plot and your name is listed with it, then responsibility for maintaining the grave and the headstone is yours.

Colleen and I tried to have the rights for Dad's gravesite transferred into our names so we could care for it. Sounds easy? No way! Famous last words. It turned out to be impossible. I had done all the legwork, getting the right papers for Maree to sign so we could have Dad's grave in our name. I had arranged with Colleen to go to Maree's. I also had all the paperwork from the State Archives as I was going to ask her about some things.

This was 2009 and I was 47 years old.

I was polite, making general talk first. I explained to Maree why we wanted to talk to her, and not even a couple of sentences in, a bomb went off.

This was not going the way I hoped it would.

Maree refused point-blank to answer any of my questions, and demanded to know how I got the paperwork. When I told her I got them from the State Archives, she responded, "They should not let anyone see them."

I replied, "The thirty-year limit has passed, so ANYONE can see them."

Things were said back and forth. Her temper was rising, and I was trying to keep mine in check, BUT, when she called me 'whore' and 'troublemaker', and came right up to my face, nose to nose, that's when my temper rose.

I stood there, but when she went to hit me, that was it, that was when my stance changed!

"If you are going to hit me, make it a good one, because if I get up, you're going down. I have had a gutful of you hitting me, even at 47 years old I am still being threatened, and now you are attempting to hit me again!"

With that, Maree spat in my face. Bloody lovely! My stance was still, fists tight together ready to be thrown, feet apart, shoulders wide, oh, and my temper was up and through the roof.

Colleen saw me take off my rings. She knew what that meant. She acted quickly. From sitting on the couch, she grabbed one of my hands.

"Leave it, Mum, she is not worth it, forget it, and let's go."

Oh, how I wanted to stay and battle it out, to get the answers I wanted.

The last thing I remember Maree saying as I walked out the door was, **"I paid for that grave, and no one is getting it, I don't care if it rots away, no one is getting it."**

Funny—lies again! I found out later that Maree didn't pay for Dad's grave or funeral. It was Nana and Pop T who paid for it all. Again, Maree and her lies, her need to be in control, and her hatred for Dad and his family came out. How can she disrespect my father like that? And how dare she go to hit me!

Colleen told me to get out, and she would follow. I do not know what Colleen said to Maree, but Colleen arrived at the car angry as well. Now, I said before that my daughter could drive. On that day she was driving, her then-husband, John's car. She backed out nice and quiet, up the street. Stopped at the intersection, and Maree was on the top step watching us.

"You got your belt on tight?" Colleen asked.

I replied, "Yes, why?" Colleen spun the wheels, until a large blue-black cloud of smoke rose from the tyres. The smoke was outside *and* inside the car. Out on to Mapleton Road and she is still going. She pulled out of it when the tail of the car started to drift across the road and there was a car coming towards us.

People were clapping and waving on the footpath. Oh, if only those people knew what both of us had just been through!

The Nambour Lawn Cemetery is four kilometres from Maree's house. When we pulled up at the cemetery, Colleen checked the tyres. They were so hot that stones were in stuck in them, and even they were hot! Those tyre marks stayed on the road for years, so every time Maree drove out, she saw them.

Well, needless to say, we never got Dad's grave in our name, and I got no questions answered. Just a lot of verbal abuse and name-calling. I did contact the cemetery manager and let him know how we went. I was told by him that Maree was going to receive a letter notifying her that the grave and headstone needed attention, and if the council did it she would be billed for it.

Left Standing At The Fence

That was the last time that I have been up to Dad's grave, but what was the real 'nail in the coffin' was Nana's and Pop's headstone. Pop bought a double plot. The beautiful blue marble headstone had Pop on one side, and Nana was supposed to be on the other.

What I saw upset me *so* much. How could Maree do that to her parents? The beautiful blue marble looked disgusting. The new engraving was done *over* the old engraving. Plus, to add insult to injury, the headstone has date of birth, date of death, family information and some flowers inscribed into it.

Dad's headstone has name and date of death only.

Seeing Nana's and Pop's headstone made me so mad, that I just sat next to Dad's and cried. Why treat Dad like this? Why be so disrespectful to Dad, Pop, and Nana?

I have only been to Nambour two or three times since this all happened. Nambour, my hometown, where my family home is, accommodation if I am in need, a bed for the night. It's gone, has been for a long time. And that hurts, because it's been home to my sisters and my kids.

I only saw Maree a few times after that day, and each time you could cut the air with a knife, the atmosphere was so icy. To avoid any fighting I was so careful in what I said to her then.

The last picture I have of my Dad's headstone, taken after I washed it to clean it up. I have not been back to Dad's grave since 2009.

My Grandparent's grave. The new metal plaque has been placed over the original decorative headstone.

TWENTY ONE | 2009 to 2010

In 2009, out of the blue I got a phone call from Rachel to say she was now living in Toowoomba and had been there for a few months. She and her husband had split up. She asked us if we would like to come up and meet our granddaughter. Of course, we would love to meet her!

Liza was gorgeous, just like a doll. I have seen her only two or three times since she was born.

I had not seen, or spoken to, Tony for a long time, so I was nervous about going up and seeing Rachel, as I didn't want to run into him. We took a few things up to help Rachel, I hate turning up empty-handed, especially with her on the single mother's pension.

Rachel had not changed: still loud, still in charge, and still *I* do not know anything.

Liza was shy, but she went to Brian. Hey, was this saying something about me? My own grandchild did not want to come to me at first, but as time went on Liza did come to me. We stayed for a while and then we headed home.

All my kids have their own lives. There is an old saying, 'You are responsible for your own actions'. Ha, it is easier to blame Mum. Telephone calls between

Colleen and Rachel and me were *to the point* now: yes, no. Calls to CJ were here and there. Rather hardly ever. We would help Colleen with Kelly and Beau. Kelly and Beau loved coming down to Nana's and Pop's. Of course, Poppa would give them things, like lollies, little games.

Later in the year Rachel had to come to Brisbane for something. It was getting close to December, so I said, "Why don't you come and celebrate Christmas with Mum and Brian?"

No way. Okay, she agreed to come *after* Christmas.

After many phone calls, we went up to pick up Rachel and Liza to come and stay with us for approximately a week. We were heading to Toowoomba and, as it had been raining for days, some of the roads had minor flooding. We had to drive through a bit of water at one of the intersections on the way, but thankfully it wasn't too deep.

We arrived at Rachel's, and I tried to help her. I could not do anything right. Oh, I hope this is not going to be what the week is going to be like. We got home, and as we lived in a two-storey unit, I was frightened of Liza falling down the fifteen steps between floors. They were carpeted but that did not matter.

"She won't fall, stop worrying," Rachel yelled at me. The unit was the second in a row of six. We had an outdoor area out the back, and as it was summer we would often sit out there; plus, as Brian and I were smokers, it was the only place we could smoke.

Rachel would come outside, swearing, and talking loudly. I lost count of how many times I asked her to stop swearing and to quieten down. Rachel ignored my requests, she was going to do as she wanted, and if people did not like it — too bad. Yes, she is my daughter, but there are rules about renting, and you must consider your neighbour's peace and quiet.

All Rachel did was sit down or lay down on the couch and be on the computer. We offered to look after Liza for her as she had to go into the city, but no, we were not allowed to look after her. What is wrong with me? I am Liza's grandmother!

By now my nerves were shot, I was walking on eggshells in my home — in my own home — frightened to say or do the wrong thing, as well as feeling totally embarrassed by Rachel's actions.

Rachel did give me some relief when she went into the city, and she did this on two occasions. Rachel was talking to a bloke, and she asked me if he could come and stay so they could get to know one another. Call me old-fashioned, but I was not going to have some man I did not know come and stay in my home just for Rachel to see him.

Boy, was I crucified for that!

"He hasn't got a car or licence, how am I supposed to meet him, and we can't go to his place."

I could not say, 'I don't care', otherwise it would have been worse than it was. I am sure the neighbour's heard every word. In the end she went out with Liza for a full day to meet this man. Poor Liza was so tired and cranky when they got home.

Rachel would sit for hours on her laptop. No way was she getting on my computer. I thought she had her own internet service. No, she was on my internet connection. I didn't realize this until about three days after she had gone home, I received an email saying I had used up 75% of my data.

In the whole time I have had the internet connected I have not even used up to 50% of my allowance each month. I could not believe the email. When I checked the usage chart, I was astounded by the amount of time she had been on her laptop while she was at my place.

Now, my allowance for the internet was 50 GB, and for me that is ample. But for her to use the amount she did, I couldn't believe it. I rang her just to check whether she was on my internet or hers. Yes, she was on mine. I did the wrong thing by saying, "When you were down here for the week you used up about 75% of my internet data."

Oh, didn't I get yelled at and verbally abused. I don't remember how many times I hung up the phone, because I was sick of being told I knew nothing, I didn't love her, I didn't want her, and on … and on.

After that, I spoke to Rachel only a few times, and I never saw Liza again.

Rachel always complained to me about the past and how I had abandoned them. I have repeatedly told them what *actually* happened, but all three of my children believe I abandoned them.

When I go shopping it hurts to see new mums with their own mothers, and the glow on the grandmother's face.

From what I have heard from different family members, Rachel has moved to Caboolture, and now has a baby boy. I have never seen the new baby; I only know it is a boy.

Of course, if I say anything to Colleen about Rachel, away we go again. Colleen has her own views on Rachel. But it is always me who is in trouble. What for? Wanting to see my children?

CJ never rang me after we visited him. He never told me when he was getting married, and I did not get an invitation to his wedding.

I rang him and asked him why, and the reply was, 'the family argument.' What family argument? I am his mother, the one who gave him breath, the one who worries if he is alright. But I didn't get an invitation. But Maree, my sister Wendy and her husband, and their children did. I didn't know what was wrong, why they would yell and scream at me, degrade me, and above all have no respect for me as their mother.

Colleen and I were still very distant, but I got a phone call asking for help, and for my grandchildren's sake, I went. But I was not appreciated—I was there just for the help.

In August 2010 I had to put my beloved Lord Jackson down, owing to cancer. This hit both Brian and I very hard. We stuck to ourselves. He continued to work hard, and I attended doctor's appointments, but my health was not getting any better.

TWENTY TWO | 2010 to 2011

Brian and I continued to keep to ourselves. After the episode with Rachel, we both were looking forward to the lease running out on the unit. I found it increasingly difficult to climb the stairs. We approached the real estate agency, and they would not let us out of the lease, regardless that I had a medical certificate. We ended up taking the real estate agency to court so we could be released from the lease.

I had been looking for homes anyway, inspecting a few, but most were unsuitable. Prior to going to court, I had looked at our present home, and I applied for it. We were at the courthouse waiting to go into court when I got the phone call, we had been given the lease on the house. We signed part of the paperwork two hours later.

I had already been packing up, so there was not a lot to go. When it came the day to move, we had asked someone to help us, and his help was invaluable. We hired a truck, and I did two runs with my car. Around lunchtime, I started to get a migraine. Great, this is the wrong time to get one! I could not stop it and that night I had to go to the hospital. Because my migraines are so bad, I must get injections for them.

With Brian's Mum gone, Christmas was not the same that year. We did not go up to see Dad for Christmas Day, but we went up Boxing Day. None of my children came and saw me on Christmas Day. I hate Christmas time. Everyone is going to parties—not us, no invitations. Families are getting together—not mine. Everyone has a fun time—not my family.

So, Brian and I spent the day together and did our own thing. What presents we gave were never good enough, according to Colleen. How much more of this could I take? I gave, I helped. I went without to help them. My health was declining, no matter how I tried, things got on top of me.

Prior to Christmas 2010, Colleen had been ringing me, she was not happy, and her marriage was over. I told her she needed to sit down and talk to John. I suggested Brian and I would have the kids for the weekend, so she could talk to John without any kids around. I continually told her not to fight or yell in front of the kids. But did she listen? No.

We had the kids and we had fun; it was great. Just before Christmas, Colleen and the kids came down and she stayed overnight. She was going out, that was fine. I told her not to worry about the kids, they were fine with us, and to have a good time. The next phone call I got from Colleen, she said was going to try to save her marriage. That is great!

Left Standing At The Fence

Sir Snoopy came into our home around Christmas 2011. He is a Tenterfield Terrier x Chihuahua. He was small and full of fleas and flea bites. He was not well, so down to the vets. Medicine and medicated bath stuff.

My boys, Sir Snoopy and Gizmo. Snoopy is a Tenterfield Terrier x Chihuahua and Gizmo is a purebred Chihuahua.

One morning, unexpectedly, Brian rang me. I could not understand him. Oh, my goodness what has happened to him?! No, it was his sister, Linda, she had passed away at work. Linda and Brian were alike, tall, and thin, hard-working. Linda had been our Matron-of-Honour at our wedding. She was the same age as me.

Brian did not go straight up there to be with his Dad, but we went up the next day. For Father, it was two months short of four years after losing Mum. We did not stay up with Dad, but we went back up for the funeral. We did not stay long after the funeral, we went for a drink and something to eat with everyone else, and then came home. I was there for Brian; and he just worked harder and harder.

I got no phone calls from Colleen for a while, then unexpectedly they started again, but this time I was worried. She had found out what paperwork she needed to put into the family law courts for a divorce, and she was speaking about moving to Nambour. I told her to think about the kids and their father.

Every now and then, I got a phone call, but it was, "You do not understand, it is what I want to do." She was working, but that did not matter. Colleen was hell-bent on doing what she wanted. Being the parents, we did not take either side; we were there to help both of them, but our main concern was the kids.

One day we were at Colleen's place, and she was not happy. John asked if fathers have any rights. I told him, "Yes, they do." It was like a bomb going off. Colleen went on with, "What about me, after eight years, what about what I want?" On and on she went.

Her voice got louder and louder, and I had to leave — I could not take it.

My grandchildren, what do I do? I couldn't fight Colleen, and she couldn't see what all of this was doing to the kids, but they were the ones who were hurting. As the days went on Colleen made plans to move to Nambour. She lost the job she had in Brisbane, so now she was on the pension. She now was looking for a place to live, as well as looking for a job.

She wanted to take the dog and cat, and I told her it was going to be very hard to get a rental with both.

"No, it will be easy. Anyway the dog is Beau's, and the cat is Kelly's."

The dog was a Christmas present for John. The cat was a replacement cat after the first one ran away.

Again, I knew nothing. Every time I offered advice, a suggestion, Colleen told me off, yelled at me, and blamed me for everything.

Colleen rang me now and then, complaining about this and that. She was going to Nambour every weekend and sometimes through the week. I'm not sure why she was going up so often, but I think she was staying with Maree.

TWENTY THREE | 2012 to 2013

In the beginning of May 2012, Colleen rang me up at about 6 p.m. one day. She had not moved yet, but was in the process of doing so. The phone call started out polite, but then, at the drop of a hat, it started.

"You have never been the mother, I have looked after you, you didn't love me, you went out with all the men and didn't care about us," and on, and on, to the point I was crying uncontrollably, I was shaking. The recliner lounge chair that I was sitting in was shaking, the tears were so bad, the front of my shirt was wet, my chair was wet, the floor was wet. I was crying and having difficulty breathing, then I heard Colleen saying in a polite voice, "Mum breathe, breathe, stop crying."

Brian came to me, and I somehow handed him the phone. I recall he said something like, "Your Mum is not well, ring her in a few days."

If anything, that did not help me. After Brian hung up the phone, he was worried about me because of the state I was in. He tried our next door neighbour, Lou, but she was out. I don't know how, but the next thing I recall was sitting outside with a washer on my head.

After about an hour or so, I settled down. My body was still shaking, and I was now sobbing.

This time she had done it.

About a week went by and I knew in myself, and my body, that something was not right. I attended an appointment with my psychologist, and she believed that I'd had a nervous breakdown, but I needed to see my doctor to be sure.

Off to see Dr M; yes, I'd had a nervous breakdown. "I want you to take these tablets and see your psychologist as well. Come back in a week to see me, I want to see you weekly for a while." At that time Colleen lived at Alexandra Hills, the same suburb my doctor was in. Every time I went to the doctors, I had the fear of running in to her. Luckily, I did not, but I was still terrified of running into her, just the same.

Thankfully, she did not ring me after that. She spoke to Brian on his phone. As always, she needed a hand, so she rang Brian. He came to me and asked what I thought. For the kid's sake go and help her put the fridge on the truck, but under no circumstances are you to go up to the coast. Thankfully, he did not go up the coast.

I did not hear from Colleen again at that time. I was still stressed, traumatised, and trying to forget as much as I could so I could live a normal life. If there is such a thing.

Then, out of the blue, I got a text message from Colleen. Oh no. She was telling my why my three kids did not want a thing to do with me. Telling me I was in the wrong for being on her husband's Facebook friends list.

But the last comment, "I am not being nasty, I am only telling you this to help you." To this day, I can't for the life of me work out how that is not nasty.

Now Brian, as supportive and loving as he has always been, had never got involved with the problems Colleen and I had, until then. Brian sent three text messages, in his own words, to Colleen. After the third one we never heard back. I do not know why.

An old saying I was brought up with is 'The truth hurts', well it must have hit a nerve.

I continue to receive help for all the problems I have mentally, emotionally, and physically. My life is extremely restricted. Because of my many health problems, I cannot do any housework, go fishing, do gardening, and the list goes on.

What I have at this time is my life, my husband, my dogs, and a few family members on Brian's side who care about me. Brian is now my carer, on top of working over forty hours each week.

After April 2012, my relationship with Colleen was up and down. We had seen the two grandkids, but after a while it was only Beau who came in and stayed with us. Colleen got engaged to Dean, and they lived at

Roma. I was excluded from helping her to organise her wedding. To say I was—and am—upset would be an understatement. Yet again, there was no mother-daughter relationship. Since it is on and off, I am choosing the off button. We are always here for the kids, but not Colleen.

Thankfully, Roma is a six-hour drive away, so we have our life here. She must deal with her life and everything else that happens. She does not have support in Roma for the kids, so she has to go it alone. Oh, she has so-called friends, but they soon go by the wayside—people don't like getting used. Colleen wants us to move to Roma, no way, we are staying put.

CJ and his wife had their baby, a boy. No phone call, etc., letting me know about the birth. Other than Kelly and Beau there are other grandchildren and all of them have been told I am DEAD. Oh, lovely.

I hadn't spoken to any of my family for months. Funny, since all the trouble started with Colleen, Maree never rang and told me she was having *more* cancer out. I hadn't even been told that she was having the previous cancer surgeries. I was not told anything. She, or my sister Wendy, would ring and give me the information concerning when, where, and for how long she would be in hospital for. This time Maree said she sent an email. I did not get it.

Life is very lonely sometimes, especially at Christmas or on special occasions.

I had a fall in late December 2012, and my ankle blew up badly. I had broken a bone in my right foot and I had pulled all the ligaments off the ankle. I was in plaster for about four weeks, and many weeks of physio followed until I recovered.

Then on the 1st of May 2013, I went to sit in a chair at 5 a.m. to have a coffee and smoke with hubby before he went to work. The pain, oh, a stabbing sharp pain, started through my left hip. No matter how I put it, stood, or sat, and no matter how many pain reliever tablets I took — nothing would stop the pain.

At 2 p.m. that day, I rang Brian to come home and take me to the Logan Hospital, I couldn't take the pain any longer. On the 2nd and 3rd of May I went to the doctors and then to Logan Hospital by ambulance. Same thing, on all three nights I was sent home. On the 4th of May Brian took me into Princess Alexandra Hospital.

I do not recall a lot, but the bits I do recall are:

- Pain level through the roof.
- Being asked stupid questions, but I was flat out talking.
- I stopped breathing.
- I straightened the railings on the side of bed in Emergency because I pulled so hard on them when I was dealing with the pain.
- I told the stupid doctor off; the doctor has since apologised.

- Set the oxygen alarm off from the finger pulse monitor.

After spending the night on a small mattress, I was not happy. I not only had the pain in my hip, but now also in my back. Finally, I was moved to a ward. From what I can remember, it was a four-bed ward, and I was the only female.

I was still in a large amount of pain every time I moved. It got so bad that I collapsed into Colleen's and Dean's arms, I was incoherent, I stopped breathing again, and lost consciousness. I woke up on Monday morning looking for Brian. That was the 5th of May 2013.

Eventually, at the end of twelve days in hospital, I had been seen by a few stupid doctors who, I am sure, got their licence from a cornflakes box! But there were also other doctors who were good and who explained everything.

All I had left to do for my Diploma of Management, was the last assignment of my final module, and I had to do it while in hospital! My great tutor, Pearl, told me that—because of my situation—if I dictated to her what I wanted in the assignment she would type it up for me. Well, after telling some nurses and doctors to hit the road, what I was doing was more important than anything else at that moment, I had done it! Being in hospital, receiving significant help from my college and my great tutor, I had completed my Diplomas.

Yes, that is two: Diploma of Business, and Diploma of Management. Both done in about eight months. So, now I can put after my name, Diploma of Business, Diploma of Management.

As well as my diplomas, I received an Excellence Award. Yes, I got somewhere! I wished my Dad was alive to see what his 'little girl' had achieved, especially after all I had gone through.

On the 14th of May I had local anaesthetic injected into my hip. By the next day it was working, no pain — fantastic! — I could lie on my left side, and bend over, etc. On the 16th of May I was supposed to get another injection, but at the last moment it was cancelled. I was told that the doctor would meet me on the ward. Like hell he did! He turned up the next day at approximately twelve midday to announce he was discharging me. Well, to say I was very vocal would be an understatement! This doctor found out a few home truths regarding how I felt about his care — such as he had no bedside manner — his rudeness, his failure to diagnose what was actually wrong with me, and a breach of the code of conduct and ethics.

This doctor was a dog, and that is being polite. He discharged me even though I could not sit in a chair, let alone sit in a car to come home. However, my graduation was coming up and I was going to attend that, come hell or high water! Nothing was going to keep me from going to it.

Brian brought me a pair of boots to wear, and I got some clothes together and away we went, me done-up to the nines. It was great to catch up with my tutor and the other students, and then for all of us to get our caps and gowns. Many photos were taken of us all done-up.

The graduation ceremony started. Okay, it was a bit far from where I was sitting. Not me. Oh, bugger this! I sent Brian messages on his phone to come and help me, but with no success, so I rang him. He came over to help me on stage with my walking stick. Oh yes, I was given my special award: the Excellence Award. My tutor was so touched, she was crying. I was keeping it together until the standing ovation of about three hundred people. Holy hell. Suck it up girl!

Then Brian had to help me up for my Certificate, and for my two Diplomas. This was the 7th of June 2013.

TWENTY FOUR | 2013 to 2014

I had not heard it from Maree, but Wendy told me about how they found *another* cancer in Maree's mouth.

Then I heard from Colleen, oh no here we go, something had happened, and this time she and Dean were no good. Dean had taken off; she needed a place to stay. She moved into the garage and the kids had the spare bedroom. She was supposed to help around the house and with money. Ha, we saw a little money, but my main concern was the grandkids.

Oh boy, here we go, there was some trouble concerning Colleen and Dean. He had gone to Western Australia, and after many phone calls, etc., Colleen flew to Perth. The arrangement was that she would fly to Perth, we would look after the grandkids, and when she and Dean arrived back, he could stay for a few days, but then he had to find other accommodation. Well, that didn't happen. She had a lovely holiday coming back from Perth. Took a week or so, and then Dean stayed with us a lot longer than three days, against our wishes.

While Colleen lived with us it was Christmas 2013. On Christmas Day 2013 we—Brian and I—made

Christmas for the grandkids. After lunch I rang to wish Maree Merry Christmas. Wendy answered. Something was wrong, and I sensed it. She didn't want to spoil my Christmas Day and was going to tell me after Christmas.

NO, what's wrong?! Maree had been given six to eight weeks to live. What the hell! We spoke for a while, then I had to tell Colleen. Question after question, blame this one, and that one.

Then, this one day Colleen was getting ready to go her friend's place and Kelly didn't want to go, there was yelling, and I said Kelly could stay with us. 'No!', and with that she went and got a belt.

She came out and Brian said, "If you use that on Kelly, I will use it on you." With that, she packed herself and the kids up, and left. Oh, the grandkids! What are they going through? Will they be okay?

***

Now, being the eldest, you would think I would be allowed to help Maree. Ha, not on your life! Wendy was in control of everything — *everything*.

Brian and I went up to Nambour to see Maree. Oh, this was after making an appointment, with strict rules on what we could do or say.

Sandra was home from Canada. At least this time the house wasn't repainted, and new curtains put up, etc., *and* I wasn't told how to dress and talk. Over the years, when Sandra came home from overseas, Maree would clean the house and tell me what to do, and how to talk, and even to the point of when I could come up to the house. Yep, everything was about Sandra, and I wasn't good enough to see her. Even though we were not close, I was pushed out even more.

When we went up to Nambour, Sandra had to be present the whole time we were with Maree. Wendy did come up, and I asked her all about what was going on. I got told then I was not welcome to come up and see Maree whenever I wanted to, and I had to make an appointment. She was in control, rather I call it in charge, of everything to do with Maree and her estate.

Lovely, just bloody lovely! Again, I was being pushed out — and big time.

Time went by and Maree was now in hospital. I was not allowed to be with her. "You must make a time, an appointment, and I will be in the room," Wendy said.

So, Brian and I went up one day. Yep, Wendy was in the room, Sandra was there too, but she left. Talking to Maree about this and that, and she told me Wendy and Sandra were in charge of everything, and she had organised her funeral.

Kick after kick in the guts. Time came we had to leave; oh, it was Wendy who said it was time. Okay, see you later Mum. No 'I love you', no 'sorry', no 'thank you', no nothing — just silence. I spoke to Wendy about this person and that person, and was told, "No one, including your kids, wants anything to do with you. Stay away, please, for Mum's sake."

Well, we got in the car, and I apologised to Brian, but I lost it. Why are they in charge? I am the eldest. Why can't I be there with her? What the bloody hell have I done? Why, it's not fair! With that, the tears flowed.

I would receive text messages or emails from either Wendy or Sandra on Maree's condition. Then, on the 26th of January 2014 at 2 a.m. Maree passed away. I got a text message at about 6 a.m. I arranged to see Maree's coffin the night before the funeral. Oh, the funeral, my so-called family would not let Brian and I sit with them. My kids would not talk to me. Colleen and Dean didn't sit with the rest of the family; and the family didn't speak to them, or me, at the funeral.

I was not included in either of the two eulogies. The only time that I was mentioned was by the Lutheran minister doing the funeral. All, but CJ, was included in the photo slideshow. Yep, even in death Maree hurt me.

My good friend, Carlie, sat with me at the funeral. After the insult of the eulogy and photo slideshow, I lost it. I was crying and crying, both Brian and Carlie were hugging me. When it came time for the coffin to be wheeled out, I said to Carlie, "Get me out first." I can still see Wendy's and Sandra's faces. After what I had just had to sit through, and the insult, I was going to follow the coffin and I didn't care one bit what they thought.

We got out and the coffin was put in the hearse, and then I had people coming up to me saying, "*Sorry*". What for? "*For not speaking up about what Maree was doing to you. We knew.*" Okay, thanks for coming. Yes, people of all different occupations knew, and they did not say a word.

Maree had said 'no wake'. Ha, Sandra organised a wake at the Woombye Hotel. I only found out about it because an uncle asked me, and then he quickly said, "Sorry, you are not allowed, and everyone is not supposed to tell you."

Wendy interrupted my conversation with my uncle to let me know they were heading to the grave site, and was I coming? NO, I have never been to Maree's grave and will never go there. Yes, I have seen a picture of it online and her headstone has all the usual information on it. It looks like a book and it is decorated with two gum tree branches showing the gumnuts and leaves. **BLOODY FUCKING** lovely. Dad's and Nana's and Pop Daetz's headstones are very basic, but her headstone really flash. But while I have breathe in me I will never ever visit her grave; I don't want anything to do with it at all.

Colleen came up to me. She asked me if I was okay. "No, but I will get there." She had been asked if she was going to the wake, and she was told I was not allowed. Hmm, she was going, but she was not happy about me not being asked or included. Apparently, she did her block, apparently it got really heated and words were said, to the point that the uncle who had invited me to the wake had to settle her down. Time has gone on and I have just put that to bed. But the hurt is still there.

Now hell starts. What is in the will? I knew that Maree had a solicitor as the executor. I saw a solicitor regarding the past family history and what to do if I was out of the will. Okay, if I was not in the will or did not get an equal third share, I had advice and I knew what to do. I never said a word to either of my sisters. The only person who knew was Brian. Wendy sent me an email saying, yes, it was equal thirds.

Well, if you call it equal thirds. After being demanded to attend the house on a certain day, and threatened if I didn't come up everything would be sold, we went up. Just great, they had been through the house and Maree's belongings, and taken stuff. Maree had not passed away twenty-four hours and Sandra had been through and cleaned out her bedroom and gone through her belongings, as well as through another room and other stuff in the house. Well, that's what Wendy told me.

So much for equal thirds. It turned out I didn't get an equal third of the estate, in the end. As time has gone on, I have just let it be. What I did take of Maree's and

Nana's I have given to Rachel. What she has done with it all is no concern of mine.

So, I received some money from Maree's estate. Stupid me, I helped people, bought things for other people, and the only thing I got was a dog and a tattoo. And that was with the last thousand dollars. Hmm, I got money, and I was so stupid, or rather blind, to see what happened.

Colleen.

Yep, she phoned me asking for help. Okay, I will lend you money. To this day, Colleen owes me over thirty-thousand dollars. That includes a car, which she sold and never paid me back for. I still have all of the paperwork regarding the purchase of that car.

I also lent her money, and paid her bills, but I did not know she was also getting money from another source.

In the end I had to go to a solicitor for a demand letter to be sent to Colleen, but I wasted five-thousand dollars. It got me nowhere to getting my money or my car. To this day, I don't speak to Colleen or have anything to do with her. Even though she still defames me and slanders my name to anyone who will listen. No one comes to me to hear my side. Yet again, she is right, and I am wrong. So, please tell me, someone, what is wrong with me?

I purchased a caravan, and Brian and I had fun going away in it. That was until I helped a homeless guy.

Well, my trust in people no longer exists. He ruined the inside of the caravan to the point I called the police, and put charges on him; there is a warrant out for his arrest. Plus, while I was out, he came into the house and stole my Canon camera and another item. Fortunately, I have had the camera, and the other item, returned to me since then. I sold the caravan, as I could not stay in it after what that bloke did.

TWENTY FIVE | 2017 to 2022

In 2017 I got the tattoo I had wanted for years, but never had the money for. I now have a picture of my Dad when he was 21, on my right arm, elbow to shoulder. Trudy, the tattoo artist, who did my tattoo had never done a portrait before, but she did extremely well with mine. Three hours, and three-hundred dollars later, the tattoo was finished. Today, I still love it, even though it needs recolouring now. Trudy was great and, even today, people love my tattoo.

There is a place at Gatton, in Queensland, called Lights on the Hill Memorial. It has all the names of truck drivers and coach drivers who have passed, when working, or retired. I was speaking with one of my cousins about it, and we decided to get Dad's name put up. I paid for the banner, and my cousin helped pay for the plaque to go up.

The truck convoy takes place around the end of September or beginning of October every year. I asked around to see if there was a truck driver who would take Dad's banner. Dad must have been watching, the gentleman who took the banner for me was the lead truck in the convoy! We were out at the Brisbane end of the convoy waiting for it to head to Gatton. Dad's banner was on the truck, and I had my first panic attack—just great! Not feeling well, so Brian asked if I wanted to go to hospital or continue. Continue. Cars head out before trucks, and I was sent pictures of the truck with Dad's banner on it. We arrived at Gatton ahead of the trucks.

It was very emotional seeing the truck come in the driveway with Dad's banner on the front, and other trucks following it.

The next day was the memorial. Oh boy, I didn't realise what I was in for! As the memorial went on, the names of drivers who were going up on the wall were read out. As soon as they said Dad's name the tears came. That year I did not take flowers up.

Every year, what gets me and brings me to my knees and brings the tears, is the 'Truck Drivers' Minute of Silence'. That is, a minute when many trucks blow their air-horns. I am sure the many drivers who have passed on, including Dad, hear it in heaven.

Time went on and Brian was working, I was going to appointments, and doing what I could around home. But in December 2018 Brian and I separated, so I got a unit in a nearby suburb. It was not set up for my disability and it did not have proper cooling. I got a little car; it got me from A to B. I started doing some voluntary work, but things happened, and I stopped that.

Brian and I were talking, and we decided to work on our marriage UNTIL something happened. It hurt, and hurt big time. It caused me to become suicidal. Yes, I thought about it while driving the car, and after the third time trying it, I went to my doctor and he sent me for counselling. Plus, I had to see my doctor every day, and that lasted for about two weeks.

Counselling, oh the poor lady, she had just started as a counsellor. I owe this lady my life and more. She was terrific. Her name was Sky.

Our wedding anniversary was on the 22nd of November, and the volunteer group I had been doing work for was having its end-of-year party that night. I was really looking forward to the party, and while I was getting ready, I received a text message from Brian. I replied that I was busy getting ready for the party and apologised that I couldn't talk then, but I would call around in the morning (Saturday) to see him. In the end, I was alone at the party. Oh, I spoke to a few people, but I was not included in their little groups, so my hope of enjoying the party was in my head. For reasons that I don't want to go into, our talk the next morning was heated, with a lot of anger and me hitting the fence with my fist, but after a while we decided to remain good friends — with a *lot* of work.

Now it was summer, and I couldn't handle the unit anymore. The house Brian was living in was the house we had rented since 2011, and it was still leased in both names, so it was decided that I would move back in and share costs. At least the house was set up for my disability and it had air conditioners that worked! So, I moved back in. As time has gone on, I have got rid of some things, and I sold the car.

Brian and I are good friends; well Brian is the only 'family' I have. Brian had been going up to see his Dad, as he had not been well. As time went on, Brian's Dad moved into a retirement home. And then in June 2022 we lost Brian's Dad. At least I got to see him before he passed.

His funeral was on the 29th of June 2022. Yes, that's right, the *29th of June*, the same day my Dad died! How the hell was I going to handle this day? It was hard, but I got through it okay. I was there to help Brian.

Dad's banner on the lead truck at Lights On The Hill Convoy, September 2017

Dad's plaque at Lights On The Hill Memorial, Gatton, Queensland.
For me, this is Dad's resting place because I can't go to his grave.

A night-time view of the Lights On The Hill Memorial at Gatton

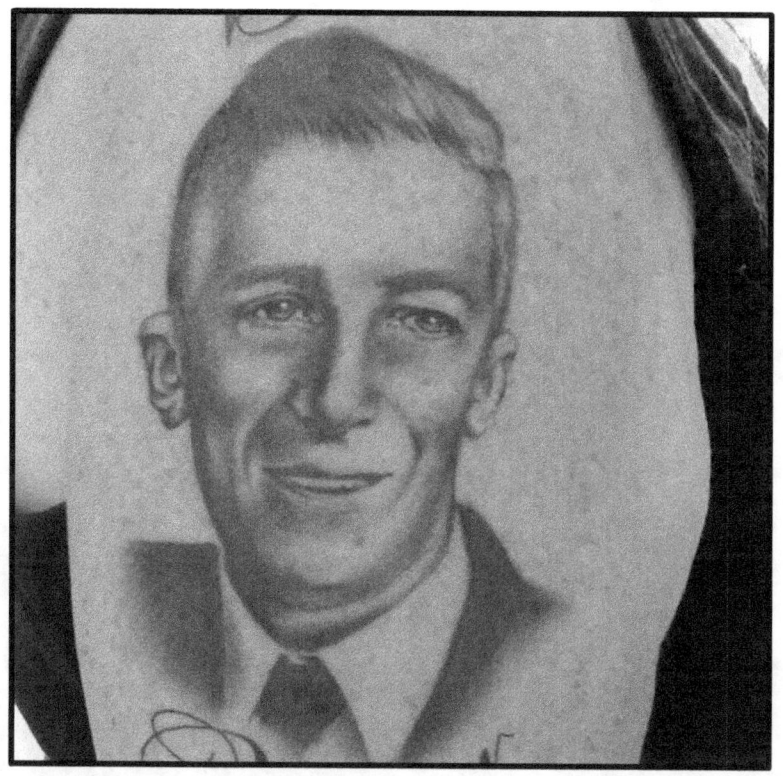

My tattoo of Dad, from a photo of him aged twenty-one years old.

TWENTY SIX | 2023

Today my life is going to appointments: doctors, specialists, counselling, or other appointments.

Every day I live in pain, whether it's from my back or neck or head. I live on painkillers to try and have a life, but I am not able to do the normal activities that are required to be done around the home. I can't even garden anymore. Brian has to help me, even when we go out, because I can't walk far any longer. And because I can't walk far now, my life is restricted. Doctors have said to lose weight, but when you are disabled you can't walk, exercise, or do a bloody thing.

Yet I still try and be positive, even if some days it is impossible. Because of my disability, Brian is now my carer, and this means he is not really able to work 'away' any more. If he does have to go away then 'the boys' and I will have to go with him.

Hmm ... if I had family to help me then Brian would be able to go away for work. But he can't, so luckily his boss is understanding.

Instead of children, Brian and I have our 'kids', Sir Snoopy and Gizmo. Snoopy is a Tenterfield Terrier x Chihuahua. And Gizmo is a Chihuahua, well supposed to be. Gizmo weighs about seven kilograms and measures about forty-two centimetres around his chest. He is nearly as tall as Snoopy. There has been many a day when I have had one-sided conversations with them, but on the days I am feeling really low, the boys cuddle up to me.

Brian and I are still separated — good friends though — and share a house; well we have rented it since April or May 2011, and it is home. The house is set up for my disabilities, and I would not want to live anywhere else.

FAMILY

Well, as you have read, I don't have any — or rather I have family, but they don't want anything to do with me, so life is very lonely. Any members of the family, my children, extended family and friends who did talk to me prior to Maree passing away, have now stopped talking to me and no longer have anything to do with me. When I see happy families or 'mum, daughter and baby', it hurts — really hurts.

I never did a thing to get what I got, and I did nothing to be pushed or excluded from my family. No one came and asked me if what they had been told was right. They took the word told to them by a person hell-bent on destroying me. And guess what? I AM STILL DAMN WELL HERE. Yes it hurts big time, and in my later years to have family around would be great, but they have chosen which road they want to go down.

I am the innocent victim in what has happened to me since I was born; I never asked for any of it, but it happened — BUT I have survived everything that was thrown at me. I am thankful every day for just being alive after what I have gone through. YES, I survived a lot, but I am here. My counsellor, Sky, told me an affirmation to say:

'I am wanted, I am needed, I deserve to be here.'

Yes, it's hard to believe the affirmation at times, but it is so true.

Thank you for reading my book/story. If you know of anyone going through anything similar, please speak up. Do not ignore them, even help them if you can.

If my story has opened old wounds for you, please seek help. It was never my intention to frighten anyone, quite the opposite — to help people. To show there is life after abuse, etc. It takes time, and with the right support network you **can** get through it. The first step of your journey to healing is to reach out for help. The first step is the hardest, but when you take that step your journey to healing has started. Mine has been a long one and it is still going, but today I am not the person I was, let's say, back between 1970 — 2000. I am stronger today, but I am still working on it.

I wish someone had spoken up when I was a child, as my life would have been different.

Again, these are MY memories. Yes, MY memories.

Good and bad ones.

One thing I will never take away from Maree, she was a fantastic nurse, very knowledgeable, and caring. She taught many a doctor a thing or two, saved many people, and in the later years Maree became a Wound Care Nurse. Some of the things she had to treat, well, let us say you needed a bloody strong stomach for it. Maree was not a mother to **ME, BUT** Maree was a fantastic nurse. Her nursing knowledge and her expertise are missed greatly in the nursing sector.

RIP Daddy.

Me and Brian today — great friends

TWENTY SEVEN | Reflections

Boy, my life has been filled with some positive things, BUT there were many negative things, too: from the mistreatment from Maree to the struggles in my teenage years, to the abuse from other people, and through to now.

As a child, as a teenager, and as an adult I felt I was given no love, no compassion, and no respect from Maree. And not having the skills to meet people or keep friendships took its toll on me—but there were positive lessons to be learned too.

Reflecting on my childhood years: After the treatment I received as a child—from Maree and other family members—I rebelled because I just didn't know what else to do. I wondered *if I was good enough*; I wondered *if I was wanted*. The answer to both those questions is *yes*, because somehow, I got through it all.

When Dad was alive the love I got from him was the love I wish Maree had given me. There was always a laugh, a pat on the head or a cuddle from Dad. It is funny, since I started the journey of writing this book little memories have come back to me. Like when Dad would leave to go on the road, I would get, "Love you," and a cuddle and kiss on the forehead from him.

In Townsville before the shit hit the fan, Dad was so loving, and so caring in his own way. I got the cuddles, words spoken with love and compassion, but mostly care. I still miss Dad's little cuddles.

My grandparents—Maree's parents Con and Olive—there were little to no cuddles, or love said, *but* there was care in different ways. Pop was just a talker; I can't ever remember a cuddle from Pop. Remember, they were brought up back in the early 1900s when the way love was shown is different from now.

Pop and Nana T, oh my, love, compassion and care were shown by both of them. You couldn't ask for better grandparents. Pop had his little sayings, like he would always say, "See you later, kid," while Nana was a kiss and cuddle and, "You be good," when we would leave.

Reflecting on my teenage years: With no love and no guidance shown to me by Maree I found life hard. I was still rebelling, but now it was because of the loss of my Dad. I guess it was a survival strategy that got me through the darkest days. I tried to reach out for help, but often there was no one there.

When I got my job on the farm I was on my own, but now I was working for someone who talked to me, taught me things, and I was learning how to get on with other people. Farm work was hard: early mornings and 'go' all day, milk the cows of an afternoon, then night-time to sleep. Until I started the relationship with Tony, I didn't have—or rather I was not taught—how to talk to men, what to do in a relationship or even about sex. Yes, I was told nothing, so you can imagine what the first time was like!

But working alongside the bosses and farmhands, I soon learnt how to do things, how to fix things, how to solve problems myself, and I was learning about mateship. Yes, I was slowly learning how to have a mate, a friend, a workmate. Sometimes things didn't work out, but thanks to the great people on the farm I did get some help with how to navigate friendships. The bosses and the farmhands knew about my life and what I had been through, but not to the extent that is written in this book. I miss the days on the farm, the sunrises, the cattle, the sunsets, and even the atmosphere of the dairy and the shows. Leading up to the shows was hard work: cleaning, polishing, grooming, leading all different cattle, but I loved it. On the farm I was told, "You are more a bloke than a woman." Why? Because I got in and did things, no matter what they were.

Reflecting on my adult years: Boy, I can't believe I survived to today with everything that I went through: the marriages, yes, the three of them, the birth of my children, and Maree again, learning about all the lies, and how controlling Maree was. Yet she was out of reach to be held accountable for all she did to me and how it has affected my life. But part of my healing is looking forward, not back at the hurt and blame.

The turning point came when I made the decision to ask for help. I knew I could not turn my life around without professional guidance and support. I had to work hard at it, and it took a long time, but I am still here. I *am* a survivor. I have learned that the greatest personal growth happens after facing the toughest challenges.

When I met Carlie, well, she showed me life, yes life. How to have fun, how to dance, how to have a friend for life. We both had our ups and downs, but we were there for one another no matter what. Carlie wiped many a tear away and she listened to me when I was upset over different things that happened. The greatest honour Carlie gave me was to be Matron-of-Honour at her wedding. Carlie and I are still friends today. Even though we live some distance apart, we are there for one another.

Just like my other friend, Ruby. We are so alike, we think the same, have the same temper, same thoughts, same likes and more, yet we still have our own interests. Ruby taught me many things; I don't wish to list them all, but the funniest was I had never been to a show, and one night a group of her friends were going to see Manpower at the old Mooloolaba Hotel. Ruby turned up, "Get dressed, you are coming out with me." Well Ruby and I still joke and laugh at what I was like. She said I was red in the face all the time. Also, like the night she held a hen's party and a stripper turned up. Today she still laughs at what I was like and when the guy sat on my lap, well you can guess how I was. Ruby introduced me to another side of life that is the norm, but I had never been told or introduced to it before.

Brian's love, his care, his understanding, and more, have been so valuable to me throughout the years. His support and encouragement have helped me to get my book written, and it means so much to me. I could not have completed the book without his encouragement, even when I was second-guessing myself if I could write a book at all. Many a night I spent on the computer, he would come in and say "Enough, it's past midnight, turn it off." He was always worried about my health, especially my neck and my back, from sitting so long at the computer, so he would come in and say, "Break time."

It has taken many hours of sitting at the computer, wearing out two keyboards, and many a time swearing because I couldn't spell a word or get a sentence right, and Brian was there to help me.

Where my depression, PTSD, body conflict issues, and all my health problems are concerned, Brian has — and still is — there on the good days, and on my bad days, and on the blackest days. Body conflict issues are the hardest to deal with, but Brian is there all the time helping me to cope with it. It is going to take a long time for me to get on top of this issue, *but each day forward is another step in the right direction.*

But guess what, I am still here, still alive, and breathing.

So, what worked for me?

From my very first counselling session I learned I am not responsible for what has happened to me, but I am responsible for healing and moving forward. "Don't think of the past," now that is hard, but writing this book I feel a weight taken off my shoulders. Healing from *all* that has happened to me will take time. Unfortunately, there is no switch that I can flick to heal from sixty-odd years of abuse, etc., but I reached out for help, and I got help. It has not been an easy road, but I am putting in to practise what I have been taught. Positive: think it; surround yourself with positive people; you are still alive.

That's the biggest thing to me, I am still alive.

One thing that helps me is to sit and visualise the surf rolling in. Every time a wave crashes down and goes back out to sea it is taking a negative thought or a bad memory with it. I love the beach, and when I can—and it is not often—I love to just sit on the beach, feel the wind, breathe in the air, and take in the all the smells from the ocean. I look out to see that wave taking the negative thought or the bad memory out to sea. Water has always had a calming effect on me.

A positive thing in a world of negativity.

As hard as the healing journey is, I want to be as normal as I can be, but unfortunately, I will not be 'normal'. I am scared, yes, but with all the skills I have been taught I can look towards having *some type of normality*. One of the hardest things—that stops me feeling normal—are the bad days with my health. On those days I just listen to music, watch television or sleep. There is nothing else I can do then, but I am still alive.

I have found peace in what I do, and that's not to say my coping skills will work for everyone, but they are worth trying if you find yourself struggling the way I HAVE BEEN.

Looking forward is not easy for me so I deal with today, and today only: Making today the best it can be.

One thing that helped me the most was repeating the affirmation given to me by my mental health clinician, Sky. Saying this affirmation over and over helped me with everything, particularly with depression, and my body-image conflict issues.

> *'I am wanted, I am needed, I deserve to be here.'*
>
> *'I am wanted, I am needed, I deserve to be here.'*
>
> *'I am wanted, I am needed, I deserve to be here.'*

Most importantly I feel now, with the publication of this book, when people read it finally MY VOICE will be heard. BUT most of all, having my book save at least one person from abuse or living a life I wouldn't wish on my enemy, will make everything worthwhile. Many people may disagree with what I have written in this book. If they do, may I suggest they read the disclaimer. **MY words, MY memories.**

So, the last thing I want to say to encourage you is …

REMEMBER:

You are loved

 and

You are special

ABOUT THE AUTHOR
DONNA DAFFURN

At the age of sixty-plus, I am standing tall after all the knock downs, and all the crap I have gone through. The good and the bad. Yes, I have had help and I will be forever grateful for that. But that help has given me the chance to live.

Today, I am thankful to still be here, I am still alive, remembering the good times, and dealing with the bad ones. But most of all I am trying to be positive and happy and am not letting the 'Black Dog' of depression get me down.

I am me. Donna, who will speak up against wrong-doings, who will stand up against wrong-doings, give my shoulder for someone's tears, and help where I can. I may be loud ... but that's me. I may be cuddly, but that's me too!

I am me. A survivor.

ACKNOWLEDGEMENTS

Publishing this book would not have been possible without the encouragement, support, and assistance of others.

Chris Elmore from Shutter Shock Photography, Brisbane, for generously allowing the use of his 'Lights On The Hill Trucking Memorial' image. Chris deserves recognition for the great work he has done every year in photographing the Lights On The Hill annual convoy, as well as other trucking-related events.

My publisher, Deborah Fay at Disruptive Publishing, for publishing my book.

Nambour Heights Bowls Club and the Sunshine Coast Regional Council. To this day, Nambour Heights Bowls Club maintains the club, and the green dedicated to my pop, Con Daetz; and the Sunshine Coast Council cares for the *Con and Olive Daetz Park*. Both entities deserve recognition and acknowledgement for preserving these tributes to my grandparents.

Every counsellor I have seen through the years — there are too many to name them individually — but I do want to make special mention of Sky for listening to me, accepting me for who I am, and for putting up with the swearing!

Lights on the Hill Memorial Committee at Gatton, Queensland for all the hard work they do in organising the yearly convoy, and also for maintaining the memorial. All the work you do helps families to honour their loved ones who have passed away.

Finally, Jo Scott, my editor. Without Jo's expertise and knowledge, turning my manuscript into a book would never have been possible. I can't thank Jo enough, and because of her great work this book has become a reality. Jo deserves all the acknowledgement under the sun for everything she has done to help me.

www.ingramcontent.com/pod-product-compliance
Lightning Source LLC
Chambersburg PA
CBHW051427290426
44109CB00016B/1465